ENGLISH WORKERS AND THE COMING OF THE WELFARE STATE 1918–1945

A thirty-five volume facsimile series documenting the debate over the role of government in the lives of the English people

Edited by F.M. Leventhal
Boston University

A GARLAND SERIES

THE ECONOMICS OF UNEMPLOYMENT

J. A. Hobson

Garland Publishing, Inc.
New York & London
1985

For a complete list of the titles in this series
see the final pages of this volume.

This facsimile has been made from a copy in
the Yale University Library.

First published in 1922 by George Allen & Unwin, Ltd.
Reprinted by arrangement with George Allen & Unwin, Ltd.

Library of Congress Cataloging-in-Publication Data

Hobson, J. A. (John Atkinson), 1858–1940.
The economics of unemployment.

(English workers and the coming of
the welfare state, 1918–1945)
Reprint. Originally published: London :
Allen & Unwin, 1922.
1. Consumption (Economics) 2. Unemployment.
3. Income distribution. I. Title. II. Series.
HB822.H63 1985 331.13'7 85-13053
ISBN 0-8240-7615-X (alk. paper)

Design by Bonnie Goldsmith

The volumes in this series are printed on
acid-free, 250-year-life paper.

Printed in the United States of America

THE ECONOMICS OF UNEMPLOYMENT

BY THE SAME AUTHOR

PROBLEMS OF A NEW WORLD

WORK AND WEALTH: A HUMAN VALUATION

ETC.

THE ECONOMICS OF UNEMPLOYMENT

BY

J. A. HOBSON

LONDON: GEORGE ALLEN & UNWIN LTD.
RUSKIN HOUSE, 40 MUSEUM STREET, W.C. 1

First published in 1922

Printed in Great Britain by
UNWIN BROTHERS, LIMITED, THE GRESHAM PRESS, LONDON AND WOKING

PREFACE

To pursue any close inquiry into the causes of trade depression and its accompanying unemployment at such a time as this will appear to most persons an otiose proceeding. It seems self-evident that a long destructive war, followed by a not less destructive peace, and a failure to repair the machinery of trade and finance, must involve just such a period of low production, poverty and suffering, as the world is now experiencing. This explanation is easy, interesting and convincing. But though it holds some obvious elements of truth, it is not sound. It does not go to the root of the matter. The economic experiences of the war and peace have greatly aggravated the burden of this trade depression, and have imparted some special features to its distribution, but they cannot rightly be held responsible for its causation.

In 1914 all the signs of a cyclical depression were present, a hectic prosperity of trade, with a high level of prices, large profits, and in most countries, especially in Central Europe, a dangerous expansion of credit. Economists predicted an early collapse, financial and industrial. The war stopped this depression, postponing its action for seven years. How? By an immense and continuous artificial stimulation of consumption. While the producing power of the world was reduced by the withdrawal of some twenty million or more men called to arms (compensated but partially by the fuller employment of the remaining civil populations), the destruction and extravagence of war raised the level of consumption far above the pre-war level. Even after the war, the high rate of public and private consumption kept in full employment for several years the fighting men as they returned to productive occupations. Then the postponed depression came, with all those special characteristics upon which so many critics wrongly fasten as the sole source of the trouble.

Now the chief economic lesson which the war should teach relates to the power of high consumption to maintain production. This it teaches by an extreme case. The artificially enhanced consumption of these seven years not merely postponed the depression that was due, but kept the available productive powers of capital and labour in every belligerent and neutral country fully and continuously employed. The destruction and extravagence of war, of course, exceeded the strained productivity of the belligerents, leaving them at its close with reduced capital resources of their own, and heavily in debt to neutrals whose surplus produce they had borrowed to enhance their war-consumption. This excessive rate of consumption could perhaps not have continued indefinitely, even had the neutral world been willing and able to continue handing over their surplus produce in the hope of eventual repayment.

But the war made it evident that the quantity of slack normally present in the operation of the economic system was far greater than had been supposed, and far exceeded the accepted measurements of 'unemployment.' Under the stimulus of high consumption the system showed hitherto undisclosed powers of productivity. War production involved, indeed, an excessive and often injurious strain upon the human factor; and war-consumption is the worst of all consumptions, destroying as it does the potential instruments of future production. But so manifest was the stimulation of production under the spur of extravagent consumption, as to evoke the thought that a higher normal range of consumption than actually prevails might maintain a higher normal level of production, thus averting the waste of cyclical depressions. If, say, consumption could be maintained at three-fourths of the high war standard, and could be applied productively to enhance the future efficiency of the human instrument, instead of being applied destructively, it would seem that trade fluctuations might disappear, by a policy which would not merely avert unemployment (outside the minor requirements of economic elasticity), but would furnish the economic conditions for a continually increasing productivity, with a corresponding rise in the general standards of consumption.

This is the thesis I propose to establish in these chapters. For convenience of readers, I will reduce it to a series of dogmatic propositions.

Full regular employment of the factors of production demands the maintenance of a proper proportion between the production of consumable commodities and that of capital goods, that proportion varying, of course, with changes in methods of production. In other words, there exists at any given time an economically sound ratio between spending and saving. Excessive spending (as in the war) encroaches on saved capital, and impairs future productivity. Excessive saving operates, through deficient demand for commodities, to slacken the sinews of production and produce more capital goods than are able to be put to full productive use.

The current distribution of income throughout the industrial world tends normally to evoke a rate of saving and capital creation that is excessive, in this sense. For whereas, under a fairly equal distribution of income, the average pressure of growing human needs for satisfaction will keep a right adjustment between the immediate satisfaction of spending and the postponed satisfaction of saving, under the present unequal and inequitable distribution no such adjustment is maintained. On the contrary, a large part of the surplus unearned income of the rich is found to be excessive, even for purposes of luxurious and wasteful consumption, and accumulates automatically to form an investment fund of capital which is larger than is required, in order to help maintain the growing volume of consumption in the economic world. This excess in capital formation is attested not only by the cut-throat competition and the organised restriction of output which alternate in modern capitalism, but by the normal under-employment both of capital and labour in the industrial system, as well as by the more signal wastes of cyclical depressions.

If the surplus income of the rich which produces this congestion and these stoppages were absorbed, either by the increasing share of the workers, or by the needs and uses of an enlightened State, or by both, this economic disease would be remedied. A sound distribution, thus attained, would react in fuller, more regular, and more productive activity throughout the economic system, imparting an order and a progress to society not otherwise attainable.

The thesis is no new one. It has a considerable history in the course of modern economic thought. But it has almost always been vitiated by some extremity of statement or by association with attacks upon the virtue of personal thrift. I have here endeavoured to avoid both these mistakes, and to present the theory as an essential factor in the principles of social progress. In particular, I have sought to set the doctrine in its true relation to those mainly or exclusively financial explanations of trade depression which are so prevalent at the present time, and to indicate the true and important ways in which the ill-controlled credit system operates to enhance the fluctuations of trade.

I desire here to express my deep obligation to Mr. Sidney Webb and Mr. R. H. Tawney, who have read these chapters in manuscript and have made many valuable suggestions and corrections.

J. A. HOBSON.

HAMPSTEAD,
July, 1922.

CONTENTS

THE ECONOMICS OF UNEMPLOYMENT

CHAPTER I

A LIMITED MARKET

FOR some time past the industrial world has presented a strange spectacle of idleness and impotence. Farms, mines, factories and workshops in large numbers stand idle or half working in most countries, while huge stocks of food, fuel, raw materials and finished goods lie rotting in storehouses and docks, waiting for the ships, that are lying up, to carry them to the places where they can be used to feed the idle machinery of production and supply the needs of impoverished and starving populations. All the materials and human instruments of production are present in abundance, nay in excess. But their normal collaboration is impossible, because they cannot market the goods they could produce, so as to cover even the barest costs of the production.

There does not appear to be enough world-market to take all or nearly all that can be produced, if the whole of the available productive power were used. And this applies not to this or that kind of goods but to goods in general. The most striking testimony to this paradoxical situation is the general acceptance in this country of the view that, for the present at any rate, there is not enough world market for both Germany and us to buy the numerous manufactured goods we are both equipped to produce.

This conviction is already operating so powerfully upon business men and politicians, irrespective of party attachment, as to induce them to regard the payment of German reparations upon the scale imposed as gravely detrimental to the recovery of British trade. Even free traders, whose policy is rooted in the conviction that too much production is impossible, because all goods produced must exchange against one another and pass into consumption, are found expressing their alarm lest, under the pressure of the reparation demand and the depreciated exchange, Germany should monopolise the market of the world in staple manufactures.

Everywhere we find the confident acceptance of a belief in a limited market, incapable of such expansion as to take off all we can produce. Some, indeed, profess to believe that, by reducing wages and so lowering costs and selling prices, the existing surplus stocks could be marketed and production carried on. But these generally mean that by this economy we could get some of the orders which at present go to Germany, or to Belgium, or some other competitor, thus throwing some of our unemployment on to another country. If they mean more than this, viz. that the practice in this country of a sweating system like that impossed on Germany (by the pursuance of inflation) would enable us, and other industrial countries following our example, to market all we could produce, experience is against them.

There are, I think, very few business men or economists who, when pressed upon the matter, would deny that there was, at the present time, a world-market insufficient to take all that the industrial countries are able to produce, i.e. a limited market. Many, if not most, however, would be disposed to impute this predicament to the political financial consequences of a disastrous war followed by an equally disastrous peace.

Now it is evidently true that these special causes have served to dramatise and to exaggerate the limitation of the market. But it should not be forgotten that these depressions and periods of unemployment are a periodical occurrence in modern industrial life. It may even be said that when the war broke out the signs of an impending depression were already visible on the economic horizon. Postponed by the war and the post-war artificial activity, the cyclical depression gathered extraordinary vigour, and attended by a general breakdown of the monetary processes, has taken a deeper, longer and wider shape than ever before.

But if we are to understand what remedies are practicable for this special and aggravated case of a cyclical depression, we must study more slowly the curious consensus of opinion in support of the doctrine of a limited market current in normal times and intensified by the existing situation. If we turn first to working class opinion, it is because we find there in the doctrine and practice of ca' canny the most naïve testimony to the belief. How far that doctrine is conscious and avowed, and how far the practice is deliberate, are matters of doubt. But that a very widely prevalent sentiment exists in favour of spreading out employment, prompted by the opinion that there is not enough to go all round, and that, if workers put through their jobs as quickly as possible they are likely to have a spell of unemployment, can scarcely be questioned. Whatever importance may be attached to other motives for slow work, the natural reluctance to exert oneself, the fear of a cut in piece-rates, or the objection to high profits based on low costs of production, the dominant motive is the fear of unemployment for oneself and one's mates, involving the conception of a limited market. It may be contended that this conception is fallacious, in that it takes no account of the stimulus which low cost of production and low selling price give to effective demand for the goods and to employment, i.e. that by restricting output and raising prices labour limits its own market. In the long run and for trade in general this may hold, though for a bricklayer in a particular town, or a miner in a particular pit, looking to next week's or next month's livelihood, a different policy may well prevail. But I am not here concerned with the economics or ethics of ca' canny, but only with the general opinion among the workers in all countries that there is, in the actual working of their trade, no security for full continuous employment. I am not alluding to normal leakages between jobs, or to seasonal or fashion fluctuations, or to the misfortunes or mismanagement of businesses leading to shrinkage of employment or to closing down. Behind all these changes and chances of industrial life there lurks the abiding shadow of an unemployment due to the normal over-supply of labour-power beyond the current requirements of the market. Workers observe that, if this full supply is brought into effective use, it leads in a short time to a congestion of the markets, a fall of prices, a stoppage and a long period of under-employment. If, therefore, at any ordinary time the workers in employment were to give out their full productive energy, they would only expedite this process of congestion and depression. This, I think, is the underlying economics of 'ca' canny.'

If this labour-economics stood alone, it might be dismissed as shortsighted partisanship. But put by its side the corresponding doctrine and practice of employers, embodied in the economics of trusts and combinations. What is the directly impelling motive for the formation of most of these capitalist combines? The avoidance of 'cut-throat competition.' And what else is this than a recognition of a tendency of unregulated capitalism in an industry to produce goods faster than the market can and does expand to receive them, at a price adequate to cover costs of production? In other words, combination for restriction of output is the capitalist alternative to over-production, congestion and stoppage. There is sometimes a reluctance among the makers of combines to admit that they are engaged in restricting output to the dimensions of a limited market. They prefer to speak of regulation of production and of selling prices. But it is quite certain that, since the prime motive of their conduct is to avoid the slaughter prices of cut-throat competition, the only way of doing this is to restrict the rate at which goods are put upon the market. For, if the trust or combine produced and supplied as large an aggregate of goods as the competing businesses did previously, they could not maintain selling prices at what they term 'a reasonable level.' If every market could under normal conditions be expected so to expand as to take all the goods that could be supplied, at reasonable prices, the chief plea for the economy of combination —viz. the belief in a limited market—would be invalid. I do not here pronounce upon its validity, but adduce the general testimony of capitalist trustmakers in support of the same opinion that pervades the ranks of the workers. Indeed, I would add, the practice of trusts and combines in 'regulating' i.e. reducing, output is identical in nature with the workers' 'ca' canny.'

It is not necessary to labour at great length the obvious fact that the modern policy and practice of protection draw their most powerful popular support from the belief in a limited market. Though national defence, maintenance of key industries, high wages, security of home markets, taxation of the foreigner, and other advantages are adduced in support of protective tariffs, the determining consideration is usually the belief that the productive power of the industrial world is so much in excess of the world-market that it behoves every nation to make sure at least of its own national market by keeping others out. This may not be the directly actuating motive of protectionist industries, consciously concerned to secure the high profits which tariff protection may enable them to take, by charging high prices to home consumers. But the fear, lest they should be unable otherwise to get a market large and reliable enough to take all their output, is an operative motive among most business classes, disposing them to the support of a protective tariff, while it is the main staple in all popular appeals to the electorate. In Great Britain, where the protectionist interests are not strong enough to win by their own weight, the only hope of tariff reformers is to stampede the electorate by fears of unemployment due to failure of a market. During a world depression, with unemployment in most industrial countries, the protectionist's claim that, by keeping out foreign goods, he can shift some of his own country's unemployment on to other countries, is not only plausible, but on a short view valid.[1]

This short-range expediency from the standpoint of immediate employment cannot, indeed, be pressed into a general support for the protectionist position. For, in the modern world, the economic interests of members of different nations are so intricately interwoven that the increased unemployment of another country—e.g. Belgium—must, in the long run, be as injurious to us as unemployment among our own people. For, though not immediately of such sericus concern, its injury will come home to us in loss of foreign purchasing power for our goods, as well as in the dearer price we pay at home for the goods we

[1] A full statement of this argument is given in an Appendix to this volume.

refuse to buy abroad. Protectionism, however, in its most specious form, rests upon the belief, supported by appearances, in a limited market. Under such conditions a tariff is advocated as an instrument for exporting some of our unemployment. During a world depression it will not reduce the world aggregate of unemployment, but will shift some of it from the protected area on to others not so able to protect themselves.

But the largest, most positive and most disconcerting testimony to the belief in a limited market is furnished by imperialism, with its attendant armaments and its recurrent wars. It is needless to press the economic interpretation further than to cite the general admission, that the foreign policy of most great industrial countries has been directed in recent times more and more consciously to the acquisition of profitable foreign markets, and fields of investment and development for their nationals. Though other motives, such as love of power, and prestige of territorial acquisition, have marched with the economic motive, the latter has usually taken the lead and determined the direction and scope of activities. Merchants, financiers and investors have sought every where to engage the diplomatic and armed forces of their country to secure for them foreign markets and fields of investment upon favourable terms, or to safeguard those which they had obtained by their private adventure. This has taken shape chiefly in a political struggle for the acquisition of concessions, spheres of influence, protectorates and colonies, where a lucrative trade can be opened up or where rich natural resources can be developed for the benefit of investors and importers.

This business imperialism has in recent decades assumed the same character of cut-throat competition, which, taking place among the great businesses in a single national or international industry, induced the formation of trusts and combines. Indeed, how literally the term 'cut-throat' applies here can only be understood properly by those who take account of the strictly business meaning of 'the place in the sun,' which Germany desiderated, and the unwillingness of other competing empires to concede any of the more lucrative areas of economic exploitation which they had pre-empted. Most imperialist states have ear-marked their protectorates and colonies as peculiar preserves for their own trades and investors, by fiscal and other legal terms of preference. Even those that have not formally 'tied' their acquisitions have taken other means to assist their own nationals to realise the maxim that 'trade, and investments follow the flag.'

As nation after nation, first in Europe, then in America, and recently in Asia, has entered the era of great capitalist industry, the struggle for markets, concessions and political control of backward countries, with a view to favourable opportunities for home manufacturers, merchants and investors, has acquired a growing intensity in the external policy and international relations of these industrial nations. This cut-throat imperialism rests on the implicit assumption of a limited, and insufficient, foreign market. The export trades in each country fear that, if they trust entirely to the prices and quality of their goods and to the ordinary activity of business agents to sell them, they will be left with an utterly insufficient outlet for their surplus after the domestic market is supplied. Financiers fear that, unless they can get pressure from their foreign offices, with the necessary force in the background, the good opportunities for investment in China or in Asia Minor will pass to other groups, whose governments are more skilful or more pushful in their imperialist policy. It may, of course, be said that the imperialistic competition does not necessarily signify any absolute deficiency of markets or investment opportunities, but merely the superior value of some opportunities over others. If the best opportunities are already occupied, later comers must struggle either to expel the occupants or to seize, for their exclusive use, the next best opportunities; for otherwise they will be left with the inferior markets and areas for development. But this treatment of imperialism, as an international struggle for areas of economic vantage, rests upon a substantial background of belief that there is only a certain amount of foreign market that is worth having, only a certain amount of the backward world at present worth developing. Each nation fears that unless it 'hustles' it will be left with wholly unremunerative propositions at its disposal. The total quantity of export goods available for these backward countries, and the quantity of capital available in normal times for their development, appear to be constantly in excess of the effective demand. Not only the best opportunities but any remunerative opportunity appear to be limited.

Thus we perceive that modern industry testifies, by a quite undesigned coincidence of theories and practices, ca' canny, trusts, protection and imperialism, to the belief in a limited market.

It may be adduced as a summary of the situation that business men have generally accepted as an obvious truth the statement of the late Charles Booth that "our modern system of industry will not work without some unemployed margin, some reserve of labour." The 'function' of this unemployed margin was defined by a Departmental Committee of the Board of Trade, reporting in 1895, in the following terms:

> In a period of contraction like the present time are many men who are out of work. They are industrially 'superfluous,' if so short a period as a year be taken as the unit, but over a period of seven years—which for shipbuilding appears to be about the period of the cycle—they are necessary, and were they lifted off the labour market in slack years there would not be enough men to execute the work when trade revived.

It thus appears that periods of contraction, with large bodies of superfluous labour, are not only inevitable but desirable, as providing the necessary elasticity of productive power! I am not here concerned with the accuracy of this judgment. I merely cite it as expressing the accepted view that the productive power of labour exceeds the quantity that is capable of full employment, except for a small proportion of each 'cycle.' I would add that the same judgment applies to the capital engaged in industry, the plant, machinery and other real capital. That, too, must stand idle or half employed during a large part of each cycle. So must the skill, energy, managerial capacity and business enterprise of the captain of industry.

The reason why all these factors of production, the labour, the capital, the business ability, have got to stand idle for so long is that all the goods they could produce could not get sold at any price that would cover cost of production. The fact of these trade fluctuations, with their waste of productive power, is taken so much as a 'natural law' by business men that they seldom pause to question the nature or necessity of the 'law.' But, when pressed upon the matter, they will admit the central truth, that the industrial system contains more productive power than can be used all the time, or, in other words, that the effective demand of purchasers does not keep pace with the expanding power of production.

The amount of productive power that is 'superfluous' is far larger than is indicated by any figures for unemployment. The Board of Trade statistics for this country give an average rate of unemployment amounting to little over 4 per cent. for the trades brought under survey, and varying from somewhat below 2 per cent. in 'boom' years to 10 per cent. and over in depressions. But we have here no even approximate measure of the real waste of productive power. For, quite apart from the fact that unskilled labour, women's labour, and in general casual labour, where the wastes are greatest, do not count in their true proportions in the basis of the official figure, there are two wastes of immense and immeasurable magnitude of which no account is taken. To one I have already made allusion, the waste of capital, skill and labour normally involved in the practice of 'ca' canny' or slowing down of production, due to a fear on the part of employers of glutting the market, on the part of workmen of unemployment. There is no need to accept the fallacious comparisons between the relative productivity of American and British labour based on censuses of production, adduced to prove the double or triple productivity of the American worker in many staple trades. There is, however, a mass of evidence from war-time industry to show how much more could be produced in this country than is produced under normal conditions.

Speeding up, longer hours, and more continuous employment only account in part for this expansion of output during the war. It was compassed in large part by squeezing out of the distributive trades and certain sections of transport the excessive numbers employed in them, and by calling into productive service large numbers of persons otherwise 'unoccupied.' By such means it came to pass that, after upwards of four millions of the pick of our working population had been taken into the fighting services, and some three millions more drafted into munitions and other war supplies, the national output was large enough to maintain the general body of the population on a distinctly higher level of consumption than before the war. This is not, of course, the whole story. A better, i.e. more equal, class distribution of income and consumption during these years, the rich consuming less (in spite of profiteering) the workers more, together with some letting down of capital, contributed to this result.

The large loans from America, together with the sales of foreign securities held in this country, are not, however, rightly taken to explain our high consumption at a time when so many workers were taken out of production. For our loans to our Allies and Dominions more than offset the advances thus secured from America. Indeed, official computations support the view that the aggregate civilian productivity was not reduced to the extent of more than 10 per cent., after full mobilisation took place. Now, considering the hasty processes of improvisation, the inevitable mistakes in organisation and control, the shortages of certain foods and materials, and all the other difficulties of the war situation, this is a very remarkable result.

After due allowance is made for the excessive pace and hours, and all the other incidents of a forcing process which the extreme emergency evoked, there remains a very striking testimony to the amount of the 'slack' or waste productivity which lay in our industrial system. How was this immense expansion of productive activity evoked? By the knowledge that there was a profitable market for all that was produced, as fast as it could be produced. The demand of the government on behalf of the fighting forces, and the enlarged demand of the fully working and higher-paid civilian population, took out of the productive machine all its practicable output. Even when the war was over, and this artificially inflated governmental demand collapsed, the pent-up demand of the prospering neutral peoples, a by-product of the war-economy, replaced the war demands and kept all our trades in full employment for some two years.

The immediate cause of the collapse which followed is no matter of dispute. It was the failure of effective demand. The withdrawal of governmental purchases and the satisfaction of the pressing neutral demand was not compensated by any sufficient revival of European and other foreign markets. The slackness in the export trades was communicated to other trades, and a general depression set in.

Now in this depression and its accompanying unemployment there are special factors which distinguish it from ordinary cyclical depressions. Always it is the failure of effective demand, or more strictly speaking the expectation of this failure, that slows down the machinery of industry. Though the capital and labour to make goods exist, goods will not be made if there is no belief in their sale at a profitable price. Effective demand consists in the offer of sufficient acceptable money for acts of purchase. Now the failure of effective demand on the part of would-be customers with needs to satisfy may be due, either to their failure to produce and sell their product, or to the unreliable character of the money they possess. Both causes contribute to the failure of effective demand to-day, especially of European demand. Many people who would like to buy our goods are not themselves producing enough goods wherewith to get money to pay for what we have to sell. Most of those who are producing cannot show us that the money which they are earning will purchase the required quantity of our money, when they come to pay for the goods we could supply.

These diseases aggravate and complicate the present problem of depression, and for many divert it from its normal character into a special case of the collapse of credit. This process is facilitated by the undeniable fact that in every cyclical depression the collapse of credit plays an important part.

But if we are to understand that part of our present trouble which consists of cyclical depression, we must treat these special post-war factors as supplementary to the main process. Indeed, I propose later on to show grounds for treating the whole psychological-financial play of credit as a secondary and dependent process.

CHAPTER II

THE FAILURE OF CONSUMPTION

DURING the war, and for some time after, trade was prosperous and employment full, because there was an assured effective demand for all that could be produced. In other words, consumption kept pace with production, taking off without delay all that was produced. The full pace of this artificially stimulated production could not, indeed, have been maintained indefinitely. But, if this war-economy could have been converted into a peace economy operating at, say, four-fifths the full war pace, the fighters, absorbed into the working classes on a shorter working day, producing the housing, railway developments and other work of capital repair and extension, while public expenditure was maintained on a high-tax basis without further borrowing or inflation, there seems no economic reason (apart from political and social considerations) why effective demand for British products should have failed and depression supervened. The high level of wages and full employment for our workers would have enabled the size of the effective demand to compensate for the slack demand of foreign customers, as during the war itself. This policy could not, indeed, have continued indefinitely for this or any other highly peopled country.

For a considerable export trade is indispensable for a people who must buy half of their food and much of their materials abroad. But this signifies that a world-depression, or any other world-problem, cannot finally be solved for any single country on its separate national policy. Cyclical depressions are the gravest of international diseases, and demand an agreed diagnosis and a common line of treatment—industrial, commercial and financial.

The general shrinkage of effective demand which constitutes a cyclical depression implies a failure of consumption to keep pace with production in the industrial world taken as a whole. There may be areas, whole countries, where production is active, as during the present depression. But their very activity is aggravating the depression elsewhere.

A period of depression is marked by under-consumption and under-production. But it is not a matter of indifference through which of these two gates of explanation we enter. The business world, employers and workers alike, are, as we have seen, strongly and variously committed to the belief that at any given time there is a limited market, in the sense of an effective demand insufficient to take all the goods they can produce, on terms enabling production to continue. In other words, the limited market signifies a normal tendency for consumption to fall below production. Every one knows that in ordinary times it is easier to buy than to sell, and that more and more economic activity is given to pushing wares and the arts of salesmanship, while an ever-increasing proportion of the retail prices paid for most goods is swallowed up in costs of distribution.

But in focussing our attention upon under-consumption, or the chronic failure of consumption to keep pace with production, it is necessary to define our meaning of consumption. The term is applied in the business world not only to the withdrawal of final commodities for purposes of personal consumption, but to the use of raw materials, fuel and other capital goods which are said to be consumed when they are worked up into other products. Although in periods of general depression both sorts of consumption are reduced, the latter sort is not properly regarded as part of the problem of under-consumption. In this analysis we shall confine the terms consumption and under-consumption to the effective demand of final consumers for finished commodities.

For only thus can we challenge sharply and clearly the accepted economic dogma, which renders it impossible to get a comprehension of the real social economic significance of unemployment. The orthodox economist regards all the opinions and practices, to which we have appealed in support of a belief in a limited market, as based on fallacious thinking. He is convinced that general over-production is impossible, though it stares him in the face at the outbreak of each cyclical depression. Under consumption is for him equally absurd. For does not everything that is produced belong to its producers, who must either want to consume it, or to consume something else against which they can exchange it, or to use it for producing more things which they will consume later on? The wants of man being expansible without limit, how is it possible that too much can be produced? If he is confronted with the progress of a trade cycle, the full activity in boom years evoking an output which presently becomes so large that it can only be marketed at lower prices—this fall of prices proceeding until a level is reached at which costs of production are no longer covered and surplus stocks of goods are accumulated, which, if thrown upon the market, could only be sold by driving down prices to a still lower level—this economist refuses to recognise this condition as over-production, and confines his attention to the resulting stoppage of industry which he rightly diagnoses as under-production. Now a trade depression manifestly is a state of under-production, but this state is the product of an excessive activity preceding it. Over-production, congestion, stoppage, is the visible order of events. Theoretically, no doubt, it ought not to be possible. Every increase of output ought to find its outlet in consumption without reducing prices below the level at which it pays to produce.

But since it does not work this way, it is well to inquire why it does not. Why does consumption fail to keep pace with increased powers of production? Or, conversely, why do the powers of production increase faster than the rate of consumption?

The answer is found in two related phenomena: first, the conservative character of the arts of consumption, or standards of living, as compared with the modern arts of production; second, the ways in which the current distribution of income confirms this conservatism of consumption.

In primitive societies the standards or methods of work are almost as conservative as those of consumption. Of civilised societies, and especially of modern industrial nations, this is no longer true. Invention and business initiative, enlisted in the cause of quick profiteering, transforms with great rapidity the arts of industry, raising this productivity by leaps and bounds. Though modern man, in his capacity of consumer, is far more progressive than his ancestors, his power of taking on new economic needs and of raising rapidly the quantity, variety and quality of his consumption, is limited by a narrowness of imagination and a servitude to habit which are far less dominant in production. There is in modern business a strong stimulus to progress in the great gain which comes to the man of inventive and initiative power, while, on the other hand, there is a strong stimulus to the early imitation and adoption of new superior methods by the whole body of members of a trade, who are otherwise outcompeted and ruined by their conservatism. Now a large part of consumption is carried on in the privacy of separate homes, under the bonds of custom, and withdrawn from any strong continual stimulus to imitation and competition; and though changes are quicker and more numerous in those factors of consumption, such as dress, travel and recreation, which are subject to publicity and imitation and carry personal prestige, the capacity of assimilating easily and quickly large new personal expenditure is comparatively rare. Indeed, it is needless to set out in detail the evidence for the comparative conservatism of consumption. For, if everyone was driven by a natural impulse to raise his consumption immediately, so as to absorb the whole of any enlargement in the output of industry which came to him as income, there could be no increase in the provision of capital, and all further progress in the arts of production, so far as they demanded capital, would be inhibited.

Indeed, it must be admitted that upon this natural conservatism of present consumption, strengthened and directed by reasonable regard for future consumption, the economic progress of mankind depends. It is this conservatism that is expressed in saving. The real economic function of saving must be clearly kept in mind. It does not consist in not spending, i.e. in putting money income in a bank, or even in making an investment. It consists in paying producers to make more non-consumable goods for use as capital, instead of paying them to make more consumable goods and consuming them. This is the vital distinction between spending and saving, so often obscured by dwelling upon the merely monetary aspect.

Now, if we hold, as seems to be the case, that a depression is due to, or testifies to, the existence of an excess of producing power and a corresponding deficiency of consuming power, we can only mean that somehow or other there has been over-saving or under-spending on the part of industrial society, in the sense that more non-consumable, i.e. capital, goods have been created than have been capable of being properly utilised for the supply of future consumption. This is not a theory or an explanation, but rather a description of the actual facts. At a time of depression large bodies of capital stand idle, together with the labour and business ability that could operate them. They simply represent a surplus or excess of former savings, which cannot get used without delay and waste for the productive end for which they were designed.

I am aware that long before this many readers will be bursting with impatience, because they think I am ignoring what seems to them other and truer explanations of depression, resting upon the play of psychological-financial forces. Now, without denying the important part taken by these forces in exaggerating the fluctuations of concrete industry and commerce, I propose to show that they are secondary and not primary causes, and have no initiatory and independent influence. Having this intention, I must first complete the chain of reasoning by which I trace the under-production and under-consumption, which are the chief factors of a depression, to the normal tendency to save a larger proportion of income than can effectively and continuously function as capital.

I have referred to a natural conservatism in the arts of consumption in part explanation of the failure of consumption to keep full pace with the more progressive arts of production. But this natural tendency is strongly reinforced by inequalities in the distribution of income, which place a larger proportion of the aggregate incomes in the possession of comparatively small classes, who, after satisfying all their economic desires, have large surpluses for automatic saving and investment. The great bulk of the saving, normally applied to capital purposes in this and other industrially developed countries, belongs to this almost automatic accumulation of the surplus incomes of the well-to-do. I speak of it as 'almost automatic,' meaning that its provision involves no appreciable sacrifice in current satisfaction from consumption on the part of its possessors, and very little thought, excepting as regards its application for investment.

That the large incomes resulting from the inequality of wealth distribution enlarge the volume of savings, available for the increase and improvement of the capital structure of industry, is the accepted view of most economists.[1]

An interesting, though necessarily speculative, estimate of savings in relation to incomes was presented by Mr. Ireson in 1910,[2] to the following effect:

Families with	Average Income per Family.	Average Spending per Family.
	£	£
Over £5,000	12,100	7,600
From £700 to £5,000	1,054	690
From £160 to £700	357	329
From £52 to £160	142	138
Under £52	40	40

There is nothing unreasonable in the conclusion, suggested by this table and supported by *a priori* con-

[1] Cf. Pigou, *Wealth and Welfare*, p. 354; Stamp, *The Principles of Taxation*, p. 164; Keynes, *The Economic Consequences of the Peace*, p. 19.

[2] *The People's Progress*, p. 146. Mallock, *Capital, War and Wages*, pp. 34–35, estimates that "at present some three-fourths of these savings—the total being about £15 per head of the occupied population—come from the richer classes, the savings of those per head being about £170, and those of the poorer majority being not so much as £4."

siderations, that any approximation towards equality of incomes would reduce the proportion of income saved to income spent. At a time like the present, when the aggregate amount of saving is greatly reduced, it is natural that qualms should be felt as to the effect of any movements making for a greater equalisation of incomes, and a consequent reduction of the automatic savings from high incomes. Under such circumstances my thesis, that under-consumption due to oversaving arising from maldistribution of income, is the normal cause of cyclical depression, is liable to grave misunderstanding.

I hasten, therefore, to explain that the over-saving of which I speak refers solely to the proportion of saving to spending, and does not imply any fixed limit to the amount that can be serviceably saved. This thesis may be presented in the following form :

Just as waste of productive power admittedly occurs by misapplication of capital, skill, and labour, as between one trade and another, or one area of investment and another (too much applied here, too little there), so income as a whole may be wastefully applied as between purchase of commodities and purchase of new capital goods.

For just as it is clear that waste ensues unless some accurate proportion is kept between the amounts of capital, skill, and labour placed in the several productive processes required for converting raw materials into finished goods, so there is waste if these finished goods are not effectively demanded and consumed as fast as the productive processes enable them to pass into the form of finished goods. In other words, consumption is simply the final link in a chain of economic processes, each of which should be kept in accurate proportion to the preceding ones, unless stoppage and waste are to occur. This is quite evident if the series of processes comprising the production, sale and consumption, of any single commodity such as bread, or boots, is taken under survey. Having regard to the current condition of the arts of industry, there will be a just balance both between the productive power applied at the respective stages of production on the one hand, and between the quantity of purchasing power applied to buy the bread or boots, and the quantity applied to maintain and improve the productive processes as a whole, upon the other hand. And what applies to any kind of commodity applies to commodities in general. In the use of the current income there must exist, at any time, an economically right proportion between expenditure in withdrawing commodities from the retail shops for consumption, and expenditure in maintaining and enlarging the plant and materials functioning in each stage of production. Or, putting it otherwise, saving and investment for enlargement of production are only economically valid on condition that the enlarged production is accompanied or soon followed by a proportionately enlarged consumption. In the last resort the rate of saving (in this sense) must bear an accurate proportion to rate of spending. This proportion of saving may be exceeded by any person or group, or even (within limits), any nation, but it must be kept by industrial society as a whole. Any attempt on the part of the whole society to live beyond its income is soon frustrated, for it is impossible to continue taking out more consumables than are passed through the productive processes. A nation may let down its productive plant, and stocks of materials or semi-manufactured articles, in order to over-consume for a brief spurt, as we did in the emergency of war; but even this national over-consumption was only rendered possible by the belligerent nations drawing upon the surplus accumulations of the neutral world. The world as a whole would be pulled up very soon in any collective refusal of its inhabitants to make the necessary provision for future production.

There might, indeed, be under-saving, in the sense of a refusal to save enough to realise the enlargements and improvements of the machinery of production that are required to furnish a larger output of commodities for a higher standard or a growing population.

Such a society might be said to over-spend and under-save, though it would not strictly speaking live beyond its income. Such under-saving on the part of society would mean a retardation or even a paralysis of economic progress.

This, indeed, presumably is what our economists consider would be the natural result of a process of equalisation of incomes. As under this condition the proportion of savings to consumption would be reduced, the growth of capital, and therefore the progress of production would be checked. And this seems true on one assumption, viz. that the total income to be spent or saved is not directly affected in its dimensions by the process of 'equalisation.' Suppose, however, that this equalisation, with its increased pressure of demand for consumables, kept the machinery of production more fully and more quickly working to supply the increased outflow of consumables, this would constitute an actual increase of real income, by reason of the higher productivity of the capital and labour continuously under full employment. Under such circumstances, although a smaller proportion of the larger income might be saved, and a larger proportion consumed, the actual amount of saving might be as large as or even larger than before, and, being more fully utilised as capital, might maintain as high a rate of economic progress as before.

This is the thesis which I here maintain.

The waste of production actually experienced in our normal operation of industry, by slowing down and stoppages, represents an attempt to save and employ as capital a larger proportion of income than *can* function in supplying the reduced consumption. This is to be attributed to a maldistribution of income, which upsets the true balance between present and future consumption that would obtain in a well-constituted society.

A self-sustaining individual (were such possible) would balance as exactly as he could present labour against future enjoyment. So would any group whose earnings were strictly proportionate to efforts. Such group-economy would apply a certain proportion of its present toil to making more or better tools, so as to lighten future toil and make it more productive of consumables. But there would be no tendency to sacrifice so large a proportion of possible present enjoyment as to provide more tools than were wanted, and more than could possibly be put continuously to full use in the production of future goods. But if in any society you get considerable groups of men whose incomes come to them by others' toil instead of their own, and if these incomes are so large as to afford little or no additional satisfaction by any considerable increase of their expenditure, this natural balancing of present against future enjoyment is upset. It becomes too easy for a rich man, living on unearned income, to cause an excessive proportion of the labour which he commands, but does not himself perform, to be directed to the production of future goods which he, or someone else, may or may not consume. In other words, the 'surplus' nature of much of the income which results from inequality of distribution disturbs the true balance of productive activities, and disturbs it normally in the direction of the postponed consumption of articles which, if consumed now by those into whose hand they would fall, would satisfy no felt want but would spell repletion.

CHAPTER III

THE BALANCE OF SPENDING AND SAVING

UNDER inequality of distribution the surplus of unearned income, involving no personal cost of production to the recipient, and furnishing no personal satisfaction of consumption, accumulates unduly, congests the economic organisation, clogs its ducts, and causes stoppages—those periods of trade depression, under-production and unemployment of capital and labour with which we are too familiar. The prevention of this surplus, by absorption into incomes where it would be more largely spent on consumables, would not only raise the general standard of consumption, but would so stimulate production and so maintain it continuously at its highest level, that the aggregate output both of capital goods and consumable goods would be increased. Out of this enlarged real income, a sufficent aggregate could be saved to provide the constant flow of new capital required by a progressive society, even if a larger proportion of the total income were taken out in the shape of consumable goods.

Yes, it may be said, enough 'could be saved,' but would it? If you equalised incomes, by distributing in higher wages the whole or most of the unearned surplus of the rich, what security is there that your theoretically just and natural balance of spending and saving would be operative? The workers would, as you admit, save a smaller proportion of their enlarged income than the well-to-do classes had saved before; might they not be expected, from the very pressure of new-felt wants for satisfaction, to save too little, and so check development of the arts of industry to their own disadvantage later on? Mr. Keynes expresses with great confidence the view that "it was precisely the *inequality* of the distribution of wealth which made possible those vast accumulations of fixed wealth and of capital improvements which distinguished that age" (the nineteenth century) "from all others." "Like bees they saved and accumulated, not less to the advantage of the whole community because they themselves held narrower ends in prospect." This capitalist economy, he holds, throve not merely on inequality but upon iniquity. For "the immense accumulations of fixed capital which, to the great benefit of mankind, were built up during the half century before the War, could never have come about in a society where wealth was divided equitably."[1] In fact, he contends, this "great benefit" was based upon "a double bluff or deception," the workers being "compelled, persuaded or cajolled" into taking very little of the cake, while the capitalists took the best part of the cake on "the tacit underlying condition that they consumed very little of it in practice." Here, indeed, Adam Smith's mysticism of the "invisible hand," by which individual greed is transmuted into common benefit, is carried a stage farther. For iniquity is made the very foundation-stone of

[1] *The Economic Consequences of the War*, p. 19.

prosperity and progress. Distribute wealth equally, *or even equitably*, you pull down the edifice of modern industry! For the saving under any equitable system of distribution will be inadequate to progress! Is it really true that our industrial welfare is dependent upon inequitable distribution? Is there this fundamental contradiction between economy and morals? Is dishonesty the best policy?

Though Sir W. Beveridge does not go so far as Mr. Keynes in his defence of inequality, he feels the same concern for saving under a more equal distribution. "If incomes were so far equalised that all saving meant sacrifice of a keenly desired present good for a future one, it is extremely likely that no sufficient provision for new capital would be made at all."[1] And he adds, "There is, indeed, no probability of determining *a priori* how the national income can best be allocated between immediate consumption and investment in the means of future production. In other words, there is no criterion for saying beforehand what is *over*-saving and what is not." Though this last statement is true, it is not to the point. For though over-saving cannot with certainty be predicted, it can be detected when it has taken place, and its detective is trade depression. As for the fear of undersaving, it may, indeed, seem to be warranted by experience of the use by the manual workers of sudden increase of pay. But such increases coming as windfalls with no security of permanence are necessarily prone to abuse. In every grade of society 'lightly got' is lightly spent. The very

[1] Cf. *Unemployment*, p. 63.

conservatism of standards of consumption, to which I have alluded, implies time for the wholesome assimilation of an increasing income. Working-class psychology is not opposed to saving from any absolute refusal to recognise and provide against future wants. The proportion of income which they save at present is small for quite intelligible reasons.

(1) Most of it, in many cases all, is required for the maintenance of a conventional standard of living which, though it may contain certain elements of physiological waste, is in the main a standard of economic efficiency.

(2) Most of such saving as they practise is not represented in what is known as productive capital. It is put either into durable commodities, such as houses, furniture, better clothing, and other personal utilities, or else into better education for themselves and their children, travel and recreation and other expenditure which upon the whole makes for higher personal and economic efficiency. In short, a larger proportion of their saving goes into personal as distinct from investment capital, than is the case with the saving of the rich. This application is probably far more productive in the long run than any small additions which these savings might otherwise have made to the volume of invested capital.

(3) Such investments as they make are mostly confined to provision against critical emergencies in the family economy, the cost of burial, sickness, disablement, old age, or unemployment. Even here few workers could by any thrift make a sufficient provision against prolonged disablement, not to speak

of adequate provision for surviving dependents. Saving, in order to live more expensively later on, or to make a considerable provision for the family after death, which are the chief incentives to the saving of the well-to-do, do not yet belong to working-class economy.

(4) Such saving as they make even for short-range emergencies, much more for distant ones, is costly, not only subjectively, in that it involves a sacrifice of really useful and highly valued present satisfaction. It is also objectively costly in two ways. Such small savings are seldom able to find advantageous investments, their cost of collection and administration in Friendly Societies and similar organisations is very large, so that they may be said to rank very low in the investment market. Still more deterrent against such saving is the high measure of uncertainty in the power to keep up payments of premiums or other contributions. A much larger proportion of the savings of the workers fails to mature in any tangible future advantage to them than is the case with the savings of the more solidly established classes.

But it does not follow from this consideration of the small and precarious savings of the workers under existing conditions that a steady and constant policy of equalisation which enlarged their share of national income would impede the growth of capital by the low rate of saving that it would bring about. For each of these working-class conditions adverse to saving for industrial investment would be modified under an economic order in which the workers' income was at once larger and more secure. Saving for investment would then become practicable, profitable, reputable, and desirable for larger and larger sections of the wage earners and would come under the same motivation that has prompted the industrial saving of the middle classes. Able to make sufficient and secure provision for old age, for dividends as a supplement to current earnings, and for the advantageous launching of their children, they would acquire and practise these new habits. Indeed, the steadily growing devotion to various forms of insurance among the British wage earners is already tending in this direction.

At first sight it might seem that this displacement of the easy automatic saving of the rich by the more calculated thrift of the workers would involve a higher social cost in the rate of interest to be paid. But when it is remembered that the supply price of any goods or services is measured by the cost not of the cheapest but of the dearest part of the supply, it will be evident that no rise in rate of interest need occur in consequence of the derivation of a larger share of new capital from working-class savings. For the price paid for savings has always been that needed to evoke not the large saving of the rich but the smaller savings of those who save with greatest sacrifice, the so-called 'marginal saver.' Now as the result of more equal distribution and better security the 'marginal saver' should be quite as well off and more easily induced to save. Therefore, equalisation might tend to lower not to raise the remuneration of saving, i.e. the rate of interest. While, therefore, the process of equalising incomes, by transferring some surplus income from the 'capitalist classes' to the workers, would have the effect of reducing the proportion of the aggregate income that was saved, some compensating movement in the stimulation of working-class saving would be set up. If the general effect of such a change were, as I contend might reasonably be expected, to maintain a higher and more continuous use of all factors of production, the smaller proportion saved from the greater product might yield enough new capital to maintain, in conjunction with a more efficient labour factor, even a higher rate of industrial progress than has hitherto been obtained.

But there is no reason for assuming that the process of equalisation of income means the absorption of all rents, monopoly profits, and other 'surplus,' in higher wages.

In every civilised country a growing proportion of this surplus is needed by the State for the efficient performance of an increasing number of public services, and is taken in national and local taxation. This claim of the State to its share in the general income may be justified upon the same grounds upon which the individual bases his claim, viz. that of a serviceable contribution to the production of the income. State work, properly performed, whether it be the primary work of justice and defence, the provision of means of communication, or the constructive social services of health, education, recreation, insurance, and the like, must be regarded as a factor in economic production, entitled to receive, and in fact taking, its necessary costs out of the national income it helps to produce. The notion of taxation as a forcible confiscation, justified solely by State necessity, should be replaced by the proper recognition of the State as a direct contributor to production, through the security, communications, health, knowledge and other elements of human efficiency it maintains. The State may also be regarded as the representative of the Community in its claim to the economic rents derived from the natural powers of the soil and the land values due to the growth of a population with ever advancing needs. So far as the 'unearned surplus' is not wanted to evoke and sustain by higher wages the higher efficiency of labour, it forms the proper income which a civilised State requires for the performance of those public services that are not paid by the individual beneficiaries. Such public income, whether applied as capital or extended in furnishing current consumable services, will, if levied in the proper way, reduce the volume of those private incomes which would otherwise pass into over-saving, and, as excessive industrial capital, precipitate another cyclical depression.

The equalisation of incomes, therefore, whether obtained by diverting rents, monopoly profits, and other surplus into wages, or by drawing them into the State coffers to be expended upon social services, so far from injuring the fabric and productivity of industry, as some economists pretend, will react favourably upon industry in two ways.

First, by restoring the economically right adjustment between saving and spending, it will give fuller and more regular use to industrial capital.

Secondly, by raising the real income of the workers

and improving the public services concerned with their health, education, and other factors of personal efficiency, it will react in increased productivity.

In a word, it converts otherwise waste income into productive energy. This formal argument to prove that surplus unearned income must produce diseases in the economic system, and that the remedy must consist in diverting this surplus into nutriment for productive energy, ought to have been superfluous. But a narrow theory, based upon a false assumption of the economic virtues of unlimited saving, and used as a defence of the privileged classes against the demands of the workers on the one hand, and of the State upon the other, has obtained so strong a hold upon current economic thinking, that this direct and explicit refutation is necessary.

I claim to have established the two following propositions:

(1) That the proper provision against trade depressions and unemployment lies in strengthening the consuming powers of the community, so that effective demand for consumable goods may keep full pace with every increased productivity that arises from improvements in the arts of industry; and (2) that the strengthening of consumption is obtained by a better distribution of the product of industry.

* * *

Controversial experience has, however, taught me that it is not enough to establish propositions by constructive argument, so long as certain deep-rooted implications of an opposing theory remain unanswered. Now the classical economics which held over-saving, over-production, and a limited market to be mere illusions, relied upon the operation of two automatic checks. (1) Over-saving was impossible, because any tendency to it, leading to undue increase of capital, would straightway be corrected by a falling rate of interest. (2) Over-production was impossible, because any tendency to it would straightway be corrected by a fall of prices stimulating increased consumption. Now it would be possible for me to override these objections by an appeal to admitted facts, urging that, if either of these checks operated with the certainty and accuracy claimed for it, long-lasting depressions with their unemployment would be impossible. But it may be well to indicate more clearly the nature of the ineffectiveness of these checks.

Now, as regards the first check, it may be true that a fall in the price for the use of capital (the rate of interest) does reduce on balance the rate of the supply of new capital. But this check is slow in operating, as a preventive of over-production and gluts, for two reasons. First, the new capital supplied by current-saving is a small fraction of the total capital in productive use, and the efficacy of a falling rate of interest in checking a continuance of its over-supply is proportionately feeble. A striking illustration of this point is furnished by the slowness of the efficacy of the diminished output of the gold-mines, due to reduction in the purchasing power of a gold unit, to bring down the level of gold prices. Where, as with many classes of goods, the whole existent supply at any given time has been produced within the current year, a check upon the rate of new supply will be rapidly effective. But when the year's new supply is, say, no more than 5 per cent. of the aggregate supply, a reduction in the rate of new supply will operate very slowly as a check upon excess. Now this is normally the case with the supply of industrial capital. A year's saving furnishes but a small percentage of the total in use,[1] and a check that operates not upon the whole, but only on the new supply, cannot be expected to be a speedy or effective one.

There is a second reason why this check is slow and ineffective. As regards a large proportion of the saving that takes place for investment, the rate of interest is either not a regulative motive at all or is not of any considerable importance. The great bulk of what I call automatic saving will scarcely be affected by a fall in the rate of interest except in so far as this reduces the aggregate unearned incomes. Some sort of conscious thrift, aiming to make a definite provision of income for old age or other future contingency, may even be stimulated, instead of depressed, by a falling rate of interest which demands a larger volume of saving to yield the required income. Some other forms of saving considered in the aggregate—such as national and municipal improvements—are positively stimulated by lower rates of interest at which capital can be borrowed, to be repaid, silently and automatically, by sinking funds. So, likewise, practically the whole of the rapidly increasing accumu-

[1] Cassell gives 3 per cent. as the rough rate of economic progress in the half century before the War (*The World's Monetary Problems*, p. 63).

lation of insurance and savings-bank funds is hardly affected at all by the rate of interest. I do not, of course, deny that falling interest will deter the saving of considerable classes, especially when it is accompanied, as will usually be the case, with falling incomes from declining trade which makes the provision of any surplus over necessary expenditure an act of keener sacrifice. Declining trade, moreover, removes those tempting opportunities for highly profitable investment, which, far more than any consideration of average rate of interest, prompt the saving of ambitious, greedy, and speculative persons.

Hence it must be admitted that falling interest does on the whole cause, or is accompanied by, a reduction in the rate of saving. This reduction of the supply of new capital does tend to restore for a brief period the true equilibrium between spending and saving, production and consumption. But it does so in a very slow and wasteful manner, involving a long period of partial stoppage both of production and consumption. Moreover, as soon as the cycle of production has once more taken a more favourable turn, the normal tendency to try to save, invest, and employ productively as capital, a larger proportion of the general income than can actually function, again sets in, and a short spell of feverish industrial activity once more gives place to a period of depression.

The other check on which the classical economists relied, the effect of falling prices in stimulating demand, is subject to similar disabilities and qualifications. If every fall of prices, directly due to increased production and supply at the former price-level, did immediately and proportionately stimulate effective demand, it seems evident that over-production with subsequent depression would be impossible. Why does not this cure work? Well, in the first place, the discovery that an excessive power of production at the former price level exists may not lead to a cutting of prices, in order to market the larger supply at a lower figure. It may lead, as we have already noted, to a combination of producers to restrict output and hold up the prices. This, of course, involves the refusal to utilise the full available productive power of capital and labour. But it completely invalidates for these industries the operation of our economic check. Since in each advanced industrial country an ever increasing proportion of the industrial capital and labour comes under this combine dispensation, the check of price reduction is largely nullified. It may be noted that the conventional economic doctrine which regarded a fall of prices as an absolute bar upon over-production, congestion, and stoppages, arose in an age of small businesses when the incentives to combined restraint of output and the possibility of achieving it were weaker than is now the case.

Again, a fall of commodity prices at the critical time when full production begins to exhibit itself as over-production, in the sense of inability to market all the product at hitherto prevailing prices, does not tend to stimulate consumption sufficiently to check the fall of prices. If it did, the classical theory would be justified, and a merely nominal fall of prices would serve to stop the tendency towards glut. But the facile operation of this check implies a willingness of the consuming public to take full advantage of the falling prices to purchase and consume a larger quantity of goods than before, their incomes remaining at their former level. But this is where the conservatism of consumption operates. Though falling prices will stimulate some increased consumption, this increase will not be large or quick enough to furnish an effective check upon the fall of prices. In other words, when money incomes remain the same, falling prices will stimulate more saving, at a time when more saving is not wanted and so reduce the efficacy of this check on gluts. This imperfect operation of the check of falling prices causes what otherwise might have been a 'tendency to glut' to harden into an actual substantial glut, the condition with which we are familiar at the beginning of a cyclical depression. This glut causes a considerable stoppage of production and unemployment, usually accompanied by a fall of wage rates for those remaining in employment. This shrinkage of employment, whether wages be reduced or not, is reflected in a reduction of the money incomes of producers. This fall of money income, once set in, stops altogether the already defective operation of the falling prices check. For the purchasing power of the family income soon begins to shrink faster than the fall of prices. In fact, it goes so far as to evoke the operation of a real check which eventually, though with great waste and suffering, sets industry once more upon a rising path. For, when the stoppage of industrial activity with its unemployment has gone a certain distance, it comes up against the other side of the conservatism of consumption. The shrinking money incomes are almost entirely absorbed in maintaining the customary standard of living, and the surplus of saving almost entirely disappears. So for a considerable time a period of what from the standpoint of normal industry is under-saving ensues. In every period of depression saving is diminished more than spending. This applies not only to the wage earners whose total contribution to the general fund of saving is never very large, but to the propertied and employing classes, whose large automatic savings are to a large extent virtually cancelled by a trade depression.

While, therefore, I do not deny that a lowering of prices eventually helps to bring about an adjustment between supply and demand for commodities and a consequent renewal of industrial activity, I cannot accept Sir W. Beveridge's complacent view of the efficiency of this remedy. "The real standard of consumption," he writes, "is raised by a lowering of money prices. The balance between the demand for commodities and the supply is reached. No doubt the adjustment takes time and *may only be accomplished with a certain amount of friction and loss.*"[1] Now, since this time-lag and the 'friction and loss' involved represent the actual damage of unemployment, I cannot accept the view that falling prices constitute a satisfactory check or remedy, or that its tardy wasteful operation proves that "the right adjustment comes about naturally through economic forces." The occurrence of the trouble testifies to wrongness of adjustment.

[1] *Unemployment*, p. 63.

It is the failure of the so-called 'national economic checks' (falling interest and falling prices) that brings into operation the more effective but very costly check of under-production and under-saving. When production is sufficiently slowed down, and fresh saving is sacrificed to current needs of consumption, the congestion due to over-production is gradually carried off, during a prolonged period of under-production lasting until the channels of industry are once more free to receive the products of a new period of industrial activity. There are some evidences that this costly process of liquidation is already approaching completion and that a new wave of industrial activity is rising in the economic world.

CHAPTER IV

THE PSYCHOLOGY OF TRADE FLUCTUATIONS

MEN'S actions are so dependent upon changes in their beliefs and feelings that economists and business men are often led to use language implying that industrial prosperity and depression are little else than reflections of a rhythmic movement of confidence and dejection in the minds of men. This psychological rhythm operating through Credit, the financial index of confidence, they regard not merely as an accompaniment and agent but as the efficient cause of industrial fluctuations. Once start with the assumption that the business mind is by nature subject to these elations and depressions and that they are swiftly and easily communicated by business leaders to the rank and file, the theory of independent psychological causation becomes plausible. In a period of rising confidence business men not only apply their own resources, but borrow freely both from the investing public and from banks, in order to extend their business operations. This borrowing from banks, being the most elastic form of credit, is of the first importance. The bankers, sharing the same confidence with their customers, make large advances upon easy terms at such periods. This produces an industrial and commercial activity which later on culminates in a condition recognised as over-trading. As soon as this is recognised, the confidence both of bankers and of business men begins to wane, credits are restricted and drawn in because of the belief that trade is going down, and this belief and this restriction are the means of reducing the volume of trade and contracting its profits. Thus a depression is brought on " because of their unbelief."

Now it is quite evident that confidence and credit, their rise and collapse, play an important part in trade fluctuations and volume of employment. I have purposely ignored this in my previous analysis, because I desire to obtain a definite reply to two related questions. First, what is the actual part played by credit in bringing about cyclical depressions ? Secondly, assuming such social reforms as we advocate for the absorption of surplus income in wages and public revenue, would the psychological waves of confidence and credit continue to produce their effects ? Now, in discussing the first question, I must dismiss at the outset as illicit and unnecessary the assumption of any psychological movement independent in its origin of the industrial situation. I cannot begin by assuming a rising and waning tide of confidence wholly divorced from economic facts. Although this vague notion of a purely mental origin of business confidence often finds expression, I do not think that any able business man would maintain it under cross-examination. He would always admit that the rising or waning confidence in the business world was based on facts or supposed facts relating to movements of the markets, i.e. upon actual sales or contracts.

I think he would assent to the following account

of a revival, growth, culmination, and decline of trade, in relation to the part played by bank credits.

When a trade depression with low production, low consumption, and low prices and profits, has gone on for some time, the excessive stocks which, congesting the markets, brought prices down, show signs of depletion, and it becomes evident that the current low production will soon be insufficient to meet the demand, and that prices are likely to recover. Merchants handling wholesale trade in the world market are naturally most sensitive to the situation, and they are usually the first to take action.[1] In anticipation of a growing volume of sales at higher prices they make contracts with manufacturers and other producers for future delivery of materials and goods. These producing firms, desiring to replenish their depleted supplies of raw materials, fuel, etc., in preparation for a renewed activity in their mills and workshops, require money for these purposes and for other working expenses, and apply to their banks for credit, adducing the contracts they have made with merchants as evidence of a reviving trade, rising prices, and profits, and a consequent ability to meet the overdraft. The fundamental and instrumental industries, such as mining, engineering, shipbuilding, and metals, where the depression and unemployment have been deepest, must get to work first, in order to make adequate provision for the renewed activity in the later stages of production, and must similarly have recourse to bank assistance for their working expenses. For, until the output of fuel and material has been increased,

[1] Cf. Hawtrey, *Currency and Credit.*

it is not possible for the later manufacturers to get under full way. The recovery of the fundamental and instrumental trades, with the assistance of bank-made purchasing power, is quicker than would otherwise be possible, for it causes a larger proportion of the aggregate purchasing power of the community to be applied at these stages of production in the purchase of increased quantities of materials and labour at rising prices. As these increased supplies of instrumental goods flow into the later manufactures, the anticipated revival is realised there also, and growing quantities of goods, financed with bank-made money, are supplied to merchants in fulfilment of contracts at prices which continue to rise and enable good profits to be made. Merchants, having thus made provision for increasing stocks to meet an anticipated recovery of effective demand for commodities on the part of the consuming public, take their toll in the reviving trade, straining their credit in order to enable them to do the largest amount of it.

Now the part thus played by confidence and credit is manifest. They have brought into play an increased quantity of purchasing power, and, by directing it to the stimulation of the different processes of industry in proper order, have swelled the great stream of employment and production, turning out increased supplies of goods to meet an increase of effective demand coming from consumers, whose incomes, derived from rising profit and wages, have risen by the time the trade revival has put increased supplies into the retail shops and who can therefore afford to raise their consumption. Thus put, it may appear as if the mere manufacture of bank credit performed a faith-cure. But closer reflection dispels this notion. For this bank credit is based upon and limited by considerations of concrete industrial fact. The merchants and financiers, 'whose skilled prevision sets the ball a-rolling,' are not mere gamblers. They see that the trade depression is nearly worked out, in the sense that the congested stocks held by manufacturers and speculators have been almost entirely unloaded, and that the actual available supplies are becoming insufficient to meet what may be termed the current irreducible demand. In a word, the waste of the stoppage has gone on so far as to exhibit a temporary condition of general under-production. Recognising that the rate of effective supply has fallen below the minimum effective demand, and that prices must rise, they set in train, as we see, a series of industrial activities, by means of increased credits. These increased credits express and measure the belief of bankers in the renewal of industrial activity. But their belief is based upon the actual evidence of reviving trade furnished to them by their customers, and it is on the strength of this that they extend banking facilities.

The limits set on such extension depend upon two conditions: first, the conviction of bankers that trade will continue on the up-grade with rising prices and profits; second, the quantity of cash at their command in relation to the quantity of credit advances they have made. These two conditions are not entirely separate. When confidence in trade prosperity is strong, banks will be freer with credit facilities than when confidence is weak. But even in times of high confidence the extension of credits to reliable customers must keep some relation to available cash reserves.

The last consideration plays a critical part in the cycle of industrial activity. For after a period of trade expansion with rising prices and good profits has gone on for some time, the keen classes of general business men, merchants and bankers, etc., recognise that the upward movement cannot continue much longer, and that a conservative policy requires the curtailment of orders for future delivery, with the corresponding reactions upon production and employment. But why, it may be asked, should merchants come to this conclusion? What is the meaning of the upward movement 'having run its course'? What happens is not an irrational collapse of confidence. When trade activity has reached a certain height, the difficulty of finding a remunerative market for all the product at current or even lower prices becomes apparent. In other words, markets are visibly over-stocked and the capacity exists to go on over-stocking them. It is the knowledge of these facts that makes the merchant draw in his orders and the banker his credits.

If bankers have been over sanguine in their estimates of the strength and duration of the boom, they may close down with such promptitude as to bring about a financial and commercial crisis. This applies particularly to countries where, as in Germany and America, the bank financing of industry and commerce has been most fully developed, and where credit facilities are apt to be unduly strained. But everywhere the recognition of the signs of declining trade will induce bankers to try to call in credits and stiffen their terms for further advances. This policy, however judiciously applied, means a cramping of industry and a fall of prices, first in the region of raw materials and afterwards of commodities. If sharply applied, this curtailing of credit may precipitate a crisis, forcing holders of stocks of goods purchased at high prices to realise upon a falling market whose fall is quickened by this very process, and spreading bankruptcy and ruin far and wide. Cautiously applied, it substitutes a longer, slower process of price-fall and depression, leaving large quantities of frozen credits to be liquidated by a gradual marketing of the frozen goods which are the economic counterparts, and which, if the process be sufficiently prolonged, may realise prices not so ruinously low as would be the case if sharper action had been taken by the banks. It is interesting to observe that criticism of the banks generally turns upon the related charges, viz. that they are too lax in checking the over-confidence and over-trading of their customers in the high reaches of a boom, and too stringent in their refusal of credits to support trade when prices begin to fall and a slump appears on the horizon. So far as this criticism is valid, it implies that bankers who ought to know better, share and even encourage by their easy credits in times of good trade the excessive confidence of their customers that prices and volume of trade will go on rising, or at any rate will stand firm on a high level, and that, when this faith is falsified by trade shrinkage and falling prices, they share in an excessive degree the fears of their customers and help to realise those fears by a credit policy of excessive stringency. So, it is suggested, the finance policy of banks is largely responsible for the excessive activity of trade and the height of the rise of prices in a boom, and for the excessive slackness and fall of prices in a slump. Their excesses alike in expansion and contraction of credit are held responsible for the actual movements of industry.

But such criticism imputes too much responsibility to expansions and contractions of credit as efficient causes of industrial changes.[1] The language often used suggests that a trade boom and the credit policy supplying it are in themselves an economic movement that involves by some natural necessity a corresponding trade slump. In other words, the cyclical fluctuation is regarded as a law of industrial life in the same sense as the rhythmic movement of respiration in the body or of the seasons in the year, the operation of the credit system serving to exaggerate its inevitable

[1] Senator Glass puts the matter incisively in his elaborate defence of the Federal Reserve System in the United States Senate, January 16–17, 1922:

"The truth in one sentence is that falling prices caused the deflation of credits and currency, such as we have witnessed since January of last year, and not deflation of credits the fall of prices."

Falling prices he attributes to failure of demand.

"Building was reduced to a minimum, road construction was stopped, furnaces from one end of the country to the other were banked, unemployment to a frightful extent ensued; and all this for no lack of credit facilities, but for lack of markets in which to sell the products of farm and mill and factory."

He adds the interesting comment: "Had the banks of the country contracted loans just before the drop in prices, instead of lavishly extending loans, thousands of people who are now in distress would be happy and content."

and even salutary action. It is held to belong to the give and take, the elasticity of an economic system which requires periods of expansion and contraction as factors in a healthy life.

Finance, thus envisaged through its skilled manipulation of monetary power, principally credit, regulates industrial life, stimulating this trade or class of investment and checking another, so as to employ to the highest net advantage of economic society (and by some natural chain of coincidence the highest profits of financiers) the available forces of production. The economy of use of this stimulus, a sort of nervous energy, involves not merely its proper distribution as between trade and trade, country and country, but this periodicity of high and low functioning as a whole which comes out in high activity and depression. So the conception of cyclical fluctuation, found in actual industry, is fathered on to finance, and it is held that these financial fluctuations are similarly natural and inevitable.

How far is this assumption of the necessity of rhythmic fluctuations a mere begging of the question ? One sees that they do happen and argues that they must. And, doubtless, other things unchanged, they must. But here we come once more to grips with our problem.

There is no ground for imputing any independent causation to credit as a factor in trade fluctuations. Its operation only quickens, exaggerates, and facilitates industrial changes that are otherwise produced. When after a depression trade revives, that revival, as we see, is immediately due to the recognition that current low production is insufficient to meet an early, expected, effective demand at the existing level of prices. Credit operates to stimulate the rate of production by putting an increased quantity of existing but idle producing power into the hands of business men, who will apply it in causing more productive energy to function in the fundamental and instrumental industries. It acts, in other words, as the instrument for correcting a condition of under-production, by throwing a quantity of unemployed labour and plant into the supply of increasing quantities of raw materials and other capital goods.

This is in effect a stimulation of saving. For a larger proportion of the increased volume of purchasing power thus created is applied to pay for the production of more capital goods, and a smaller proportion is applied to the purchase of final commodities for consumption. While, then, during the depression the proportion of saving to spending was kept abnormally low, so as to let out the previous accumulations of unmarketable goods, the revival of trade is initiated by financial measures which force more saving and so reinvigorate the productive processes.

Since the use of the new credits involves increased employment of labour and a larger aggregate wage-bill, a good deal of the enlarged volume of purchasing power will soon begin to operate at the other end of industry in a growing demand for consumable commodities. But the early normal effect of a trade revival through expanding credit will be a rise of prices and an enlarged sale of materials and semi-manufactured goods, on terms of high profits. Though more employment will give higher aggregate wages, wage-rates will not rise so fast as prices and profits. This wage-lag is generally admitted. It signifies for us the important fact that during rising prices and reviving trade the distribution of the product, i.e. of real incomes, is favourable to the employing and capitalist classes, unfavourable to labour. For though the wages and even the real income of the workers may be rising with the enlargement of the product, this enhanced working-class income represents a smaller proportion of the whole income. Now since saving, as we see, comes mainly from the accumulation of surplus income of the capitalist and employing classes, the under-saving which accompanied depression now gives place to what will once more become over-saving when the revival of trade has gone some distance. For as the process of revival with rising prices goes on, the amount of fresh credit needed to finance the expanding volume of business on a higher price level continually grows, and since the time-lag for wages still keeps trade highly profitable, the increased saving and the increasing production continues, making once more towards a rate of production visibly greater than is able to find a profitable market So a check upon the rise of prices takes place, the lag of wages has time to catch up, and employers are faced with high costs of production when prices are beginning to fall and markets are insecure. Under such circumstances finance begins to take alarm and credits are restricted, and so the downward path once more is taken.

Now what I wish to ask is in what sense this fluctuation, thus induced, can be regarded rightly as inevitable, inherent in the nature of industry. Given a tardy recovery brought about in the way here described, making towards a condition of full employment of the available factors of production, capital and labour, is there any reason why the full employment at high prices, with high profits and high wages, should not continue indefinitely? Only one, viz. a failure to sell at the current high prices the whole supply of final commodities which the whole process of production is capable of putting into the markets. Now it is admitted that all these final commodities could be sold, in the sense that some one possesses the money income capable of buying them, i.e. they belong to someone who can either consume them or exchange them for other consumables which he prefers.[1] But the fact remains that they cannot find a sufficient number of buyers and consumers, and, therefore, being left unbought, congest the markets and bring down prices, and even at these lower prices cannot get a full market. This congestion operates at once to slow down all the processes of production, and so the world gets once more into a depression.

Now we have noted one significant fact in the process of trade revival which may explain the apparent necessity of over-production and collapse That is the admitted lag of wages. This lag continues throughout the upward process, when with expanding credit and production prices and profits rise. Only when

[1] We discuss later the theory of Major Douglas, which involves a denial of this assumption.

the rise of prices has already stopped for some time do wages catch up, and high wages are then held responsible for the failure to market goods at profitable prices.

Now, suppose that by some economic arrangement it were possible to do away with the lag of wages, so that wage rates rose automatically and proportionately with rises of prices and of profits. Is it not evident, that we should have an important correction of fluctuations? It would operate in two ways, first in reducing the rate of profits and so the rate of saving and of increased production, secondly, in stimulating the rate of consumption. In other words, it would make for an adjustment between the rate of reviving production and of reviving consumption which might maintain an equilibrium between the two processes at a high level for an indefinite time, avoiding the slump otherwise held to be inevitable. The expansion of production and employment would, as before, continue until all the factors of production were in full use, but this process would go more slowly because a smaller proportion of the income would be available for saving, i.e. for making capital goods. But, assuming that the adjustment between wages and profits were such as to keep an economically sound proportion between growth of production and of consumption, there seems no reason why the high level of trade, prices, and employment, once restored, should not be maintained.

The removal of the wage-lag would also act in another way on credit and prices. By curbing the high profits, which the wage-lag renders possible, it would reduce the incentive of business men to borrow and of bankers to lend. So less credit would be manufactured, prices would not rise as much or as fast, and the whole process of reviving trade would take place more slowly. This slower recovery would be the price paid for the greater security of the recovered trade. The removal of the wage-lag would thus certainly reduce the fluctuation, by making the recovery of trade more gradual and preventing the level of prices rising so high. As soon as production and employment attained their full dimensions, the tendency to congestion of markets would be checked by the existence of a larger demand for commodities on the part of labour. So, even supposing that the adjustment between production and consumption were not kept true by the removal of the wage-lag, and a glut of goods took place, followed by a decline of trade and of employment, that glut would be smaller and the depression would be shallower.

CHAPTER V

SURPLUS INCOME THE CAUSE OF FLUCTUATIONS

If there are any to whom I appear to be urging on behalf of labour a ' heads I win, tails you lose ' policy, by insisting that a removal of the wage-lag is only good in a rising and not in a falling market, my reply is that I am not concerned with the wage-lag, as such, but only with its bearing upon the proportion between wages and profits. If I am right in holding that the under-consumption which visibly cramps the use of the full powers of industry is due in large part to the excessive share of the product which goes normally to ' capital ' and the defective share which goes to labour, the removal of the wage-lag is only advantageous in so far as it reduces the aggregate amount of this maldistribution. It is consistent with this purpose to advocate the removal of the wage-lag only when that lag diminishes the share of labour.

But though this policy would, undoubtedly, reduce the cyclical fluctuations, and maintain a higher average as well as a more even state of production and employment, it would not in itself form a sufficient remedy. For the constant tendency towards over-production, gluts, and stoppages, lies, as we have seen, in the existence of a surplus of unearned and excessive incomes, largely unexpended even upon luxurious goods and services, and accumulating in material capital which turns out to be incapable of full regular functioning in order to supply the consumption which this process permits to take place. Now the removal of the wage-lag, though diminishing the surplus, could not absorb it. No wage policy, by itself, could do more than reduce this surplus. It could not remove the differential rents, profits, interests, or other elements of income obtained for the possession of land, capital, or ability endowed with some advantage of nature or position. Nor could labour with any justice or social expediency lay claim to the monopoly-profits of trusts, combines, and other non-competitive businesses, whose control over selling prices enables them to extract excessive incomes. Such elements of surplus, as is widely recognised, form a proper source of public revenue

The removal of the wage-lag in reviving trade with rising prices and profits, therefore, must only be regarded as one contribution towards a solution of our problem. A full theoretical and practical solution can only be found in the conjunction of an adequate system of remuneration of labour with a similarly adequate system of taxation. Removal of the wage-lag will not prevent, though it will retard and diminish, trade depressions and unemployment, if the wage basis itself is a normally deficient provision for remunerating labour. Only where the normal wage basis gives a full wage of efficiency, will the removal of the wage-lag be powerfully effective to check the high profits, excessive credit, over-saving and over-production, which are the forerunners of depression. For a normally full wage of efficiency in a competitive industry will tend to keep down profits also to a subsistence wage for capital, and during a trade revival the increased product would be distributed between the two, more in their capacity of consumers than of producers. That is to say, given a competitive trade, prices would not rise rapidly or greatly, and the larger money incomes received both by employers and employed for the fuller utilisation of their productive powers would be realised in an increased purchasing power over commodities.

In non-competitive or monopolistic trade, so far as it is left in private hands, and in default of public price-control, taxation is, as we perceive, the proper remedy.

The conjunction of these two policies will be efficacious in checking depressions and unemployment in proportion as, by expanding private and public consumption, it furnishes a regular effective demand for the maximum output of the industrial system. This, of course, does not assume a statical condition of industry. As the arts of industry advance, a given quantity of human productive energy is able to turn out an increasing quantity of consumable goods. An increasing population with a rising standard of consumption is able to purchase and consume the increasing output. But the advancing arts of industry require for their effective operation large quantities of new capital. This need involves the continuous sacrifice of a certain amount of immediate consumption in order to supply that capital. But that certain amount of saving should be directly proportionate to the rising volume of consumption. Any failure to save as much involves not only less production, but less consumption in the near future. Any attempt to save more than that proportion involves waste of the excess by unemployment, both production and consumption being less than would have been the case had the right proportion of saving to spending been preserved.

An accurate adjustment between production and consumption in a progressive society would not, of course, rule out all trade fluctuations. Considerable failures of world-harvests, affecting important foods and raw materials, might reduce the productivity of industry, by diminishing the supply of these prime products to the manufacturing, transport, and distributive trades, and by lowering the consumption and efficiency of labour. But every rise in the general standard of living, bringing into play more fully the law of substitution, every improvement of communications enlarging the variety of available sources of each supply, every improved provision for the storage and preservation of perishable goods, diminishes the influence upon industry of these natural variations. Though famine in such countries as China and Russia, and the simultaneous failure of the Indian and American cotton crop, might still have some influence in depressing world industry, no considerable depression in the modern world can be attributed to such a cause.

An important contributory cause of some modern depressions has been the excessive application of capital and business enterprise to certain fields of fundamental industry. Railway construction with its appendages of docks, harbours, warehouses, etc., has been a notorious example. When an era of industrial prosperity has evoked great confidence in its continuance, and high profits yield a large investment fund available for speculative enterprise, a boom in American and other foreign railways has been organised to take off the capital superfluous for safer home uses. "The most common form for the absorption of capital, as well as the most correct barometer of activity in the United States from 1848 to 1890 was railway building, which in each case reached a maximum some months or years before the occurrence of the crisis or the beginning of the depression."[1]

The statistics of Great Britain's foreign investments bear out this ascription of over-investment in fundamental industries of a speculative order as a precipitating cause of depressions. This misdirection of the enlarged saving-fund of prosperous trade is natural enough. While it lasts, it means a full employment and large development of the fundamental industries in the investing country and others, coal and iron, metals and engineering, which go to furnish the concrete capital for the foreign railroads, etc. When it becomes evident that the process has gone too far, and that many of these roads cannot within any reasonable time be made to pay their way and yield a profit to investors, a financial crisis follows, the flow first of bank credits for immediate financing of the ventures, then of new capital to carry them further, fails, and an era of bankruptcy and reconstruction sets in,

[1] Burton, *Financial Crises*, p. 85.

accompanied by a complete damping down of railway enterprises for several years.

It is natural that investigations into the history of trade fluctuations should fasten attention on these speculative excesses of investment and assign to them the causation of the subsequent depressions. If our analysis be correct, such excesses must occur. A creation of savings obviously superfluous for the formation of capital to supply goods for current home consumption must cause an increasing proportion of new savings to seek investment in undertakings at a distance which do not supply current consumption but fructify for supply of consumptive goods some years hence. It is only when business men and financiers begin to calculate whether the great anticipated increase of future consumption, upon which the investments are based, is likely to come off and reach an adverse judgment, that the folly and futility of the proceeding are unmasked, and the penalty is paid in a sudden slump in the home trades which had been supplying these capital goods for the export trade.

Under a better distribution of income, with a right adjustment between production and consumption, these excessive funds available for speculative investments abroad would not exist. This does not signify that home demands would absorb all savings. That would be a false and ill-directed economy for a progressive nation. But it would preclude these speculative rushes into foreign investment as the only outlet for congested home demands, and it would remove this important factor in the production of financial crises and industrial depressions.

The upshot of this discussion of the relation between the financial and industrial factors in trade fluctuations and depressions is to reduce the former to an ancillary and supplementary position. The part attributed to the swelling and collapse of credit is both misconceived and overstated. The real importance of the operation of credit as a factor in industrial fluctuations is derived from the maladjustment between production and consumption. For it is the ultimately futile and mischievous endeavour to apply to production an excessive proportion of the income derived from it that stimulates trade to a period of feverish activity followed by a period of depression and collapse. The rapid expansibility of purchasing power through the creation of bank credits serves, as we have seen, to facilitate both the boom and the collapse, and by its reactions upon prices and expectations to carry both processes farther and faster than they could go under a system of cash payments or of properly restricted credit.

It is idle to say that the existing operation of bank credits is essential to the elasticity of trade, when it is demonstrated that excessive credits are instrumental in expansions and subsequent contractions that are wasteful and dangerous in their working. The representation of cyclical fluctuations, as belonging to a necessary and even a beneficent order of nature, is quite the most impudent of all the fatalistic doctrines by which defenders of the present order endeavour to stop the wheels of progress.

* * *

We have seen how the large manufacture of cheap credit during a period of prosperity leads to over-trading, i.e. the production of surplus stocks of goods which turn out to be immediately unsaleable at cost prices and which are only got rid of during a long period of depression and under-production due to their existence. This over-trading, or production of excessive stocks, is promoted by abundant credit, not merely because that credit increases the quantity of purchasing power, so raising prices, but because it is primarily applied to stimulate the production of capital-goods without any corresponding stimulation of consumption. This criticism is not met by urging that the credit enables employers to give fuller employment at rising wage-rates, so increasing the effective demand for consumables by labour. For the credit first operates to throw an increased proportion of the productive power of labour and capital on to the production of non-consumables, raw materials, fuel, etc., the advance of these primary products towards the condition of finished consumable commodities being usually held up by congestion in the mills or warehouses or in the dealers' hands when the boom has reached its height and depression is in sight. For a time free credit does put more money into the workers' pockets. But it does not proportionately raise consumption. For the rising margin of profits on an expanding trade, taken in conjunction with the wage-lag, means a larger share of the expanding income for capital and a smaller for labour. And this means, as we have recognised, a larger proportion of saving to spending, of production to consumption, in a word, a quickening of the process of over-production and depression.

Now if the manufacture of credit thus aggravates the maladjustment of production and consumption by raising profits more than wages, it seems to follow that any possible use of credit as a remedy for actual unemployment must turn upon a reversal of this action. If the State is to assist in healing and reducing unemployment by the use of public credit, this credit must be applied to purposes where its expenditure goes as much as possible into wages, as little as possible into profits, rents, interest, or high salaries. It might at first sight seem that this condition would be best fulfilled by a policy of doles to the unemployed. And, indeed, the first effect of treatment by doles, or by contributory funds to which the workers have contributed a smaller proportion than their ordinary wages bear to the rest of the national income, is favourable in that it places a larger share of the total purchasing power in the hands of the working-classes who will apply it in consuming a larger share of the available consumptive goods than they could otherwise. Something would thus be done temporarily towards adjusting the rate of consumption to that of production by letting out more quickly the surplus stocks of finished goods which have been congesting the economic system. But such temporary subsidies to labour cannot make any real contribution towards that permanently right adjustment between production and consumption which would keep both processes functioning at a higher level. The stimulus it can afford to actual current production is slight, and the more rapid removal of the congestion, which is its chief result, only prepares the way sooner for another renewal of trade activity along the familiar road towards repletion and depression.

Indeed, it is the most severe criticism of our existing system that it is temporarily advantageous to pay the unemployed to do nothing. On a short view, and ignoring the damaging reactions on economic efficiency and character, it seems usually better to keep the unemployed in idleness rather than to get them to work producing any of the ordinary sorts of goods for the market which is *ex hypothesi* already over-supplied. The next best thing (or the best, allowing for other circumstances) would be to set them to produce one of two classes of extraordinary goods. The first class consists of useful public works of immediately non-remunerative kinds in the sense that no business firm could at the present time afford to undertake them, and which do not at once facilitate the production of ordinary goods or services. Municipal or State undertakings for some new or improved service performed directly by the public authority, and thus furnishing a minimum of private profit while employing the largest proportion of labour to the capital required, would best meet the requirements of the situation. The erection of electric superstations, or the building of a Channel Tunnel, are examples of such public works. Though both would react in a future increase of general productivity, that reaction would be postponed, the immediate effect being to increase the proportion of purchasing power in the hands of workers who would use it in increased effective demand for commodities, thus clearing off any gluts of goods still congesting the industrial system and enabling fresh flows of raw materials to pass into the productive processes. The future increase of general productivity which these public works would yield would, when matured, not contribute to bring about another glut, provided the profits or rents they yielded were kept in public hands and used for health, education, recreation, and other non-competitive purposes.

Long-term credits, for financing export trade, with countries whose broken productive and financial resources disable them from exercising effective demand for our goods through the usual channels, could also be brought into accord with sound policy. Austria, Poland, Russia, let us say, are in need of steam engines and ploughs to revive their agriculture and transport, but cannot pay for them at present in money or goods. If they were given, on the Ter Meulen or some other plan, credits long enough to enable them to buy these engines and ploughs from us as soon as we could deliver them, but to postpone payment for them in actual goods until their use had time to fructify in exportable grain, timber, sugar, and other goods, the direct effect of this use of credits would be to stimulate employment in our engineering and connected trades, and to alter the proportion of monetary incomes here so as to increase effective demands for commodities in general. The later flow of return-goods into this country would be of a nature not to compete directly with our own product to any appreciable degree, and if postponed, as is likely, until depression had passed away, would easily and advantageously be absorbed in the rising markets.

There is, however, one obvious qualification to this economy. Its validity turns upon the proportion of wages to profits in the application of such credits to our industries, whose activity is thus stimulated. If the public credit, thus applied to this stimulation of our export trades were to pass into profits in a proportion equalling or exceeding the normal rate prevailing at such a time, that would imply not only a less immediate absorption of the unemployed but an earlier recurrence of the next period of over-trading and congestion of the markets.

In fine, the ultimate effect of credit, regarded as a means of stimulating trade and employment, will depend upon its influence upon the distribution of the general income. It will be favourable according as it increases the proportion of the general income passing to the wage-earners or to public bodies to be spent in demand for commodities or the financing of non-industrial services.

CHAPTER VI

WAGE REDUCTION AS REMEDY FOR DEPRESSION

I HAVE argued that the removal of the wage-lag on rising markets and advancing prices would furnish a substantial check upon over-production, congestion of markets and depression. It will occur to some readers that what holds for the up-grade movement should hold for the down-grade, and that if wages are made to rise in order to keep pace with rising prices, so they should fall with falling prices. This demand, indeed, is treated often as an essential condition for the recovery of trade. Let it, however, be clearly understood that the demand for wage-reduction is not confined to a reduction in money-wages equivalent to the reduction in prices. In depressed trade, with general unemployment, business men have considerable support from economists in calling for cuts in real wages as well as money-wages. The acceptance of lower wages by workers, it is contended, will curb the depression and reduce the volume of unemployment, by lowering costs of production and selling prices so as to enable all businesses adopting the policy to obtain a larger market than they could get otherwise.

Take first the case of businesses, or trades, producing

for the home market, e.g. the building trades. Lower wages will mean cheaper houses. Cheaper houses will mean a demand for more and larger houses, thus furnishing more employment to capital and labour in the building trades. The acceptance of lower wages will not mean a reduction of money income, or of aggregate demand for commodities, on the part of the whole body of workers in the building trades. For the larger number employed and the fuller employment at the lower wage-rates, will leave this class of workers with as large or even a larger aggregate of purchasing power than they would have had by refusing to take lower rates. Indeed, it is argued, if other workers besides those in the building trades are also accepting lower wages, costs and prices will fall in these other trades, so that workers in the building trades will be able to spend their reduced money incomes more advantageously. In other words, it is suggested that by a general reduction of wages the workers will be at least as well, or better off, than before. They will buy more of one another's products at lower prices. More workers in each trade will be employed and earning incomes, so that the total purchasing and consuming power will be greater than would be the case if 20 per cent. of them remained unemployed and the other 80 per cent. did short time at high wage-rates.

In other words, wage reduction will mean that capital and labour, which otherwise stand idle because what they could produce could not get sold on terms which would give even a minimum profit to the employer, can now be employed and the product sold so as to yield this minimum profit. A larger total product will be produced and sold. A smaller proportion of this larger product will go to labour, than of the smaller product under the higher wage rate. For, though the capital brought into productive use by the wage-cut may only earn a bare minimum profit, the better placed capital, which it was worth while to employ before the wage-cut, will now be earning a higher rate of profit. But though a smaller proportion of the enlarged product thus goes to the workers, the actual amount they receive as a body will be larger than before the cut, though they will have to do more work to get it.

The distribution of the smaller product before the wage cut was more favourable to labour than to capital, the distribution afterwards returns to the normal position, which is favourable to capital. But since workers suffer more severely from unemployment and low incomes than do capitalists, it may be worth their while to accept a wage-cut which increases their aggregate real income, although it involves more output of labour power and gives capital a larger share of the increased product. For, after all, the stoppage of work and unemployment were caused directly by the inability of some of the capital to earn the necessary minimum of profit, and no remedy could be effective that did not remove this inability and restore the profit-earning power of this idle capital.

This, I think, is the economic case made by capital for wage-reduction as a cure for depression and unemployment in trades working for the home-market.

Before presenting the counter-arguments of labour, it is, however, well to take account of an important qualification of this case for wage reduction. Its validity depends upon what is termed 'the elasticity of demand' for labour. Now that demand is elastic if the increased output of goods, which could be produced by employing more workers at lower wages, can readily force an expansion of the market by lowering prices. On this point the instance of housing, in such a depression as the present, is unconvincing. For housing happens to be the one prevailing exception to the rule that, when a depression sets in, the markets are all glutted with goods that cannot get sold. Now, though it be true for every class of goods that there is a price so low as gradually to take off this glut, and that a depression continues until prices have reached and remained at this low level for some time, it does not follow that a fresh output during this process, produced at low wage-rates, will stimulate the pace of this depletion. On the contrary, to produce more goods at lower labour costs will appear to add as much to the glut of supply as it does to the effective demand, so that any immediate gain in volume of employment and rate of consumption may be accompanied by a prolongation of the period of depression.

But the main defence of labour against the capitalist claim for lower wage-rates as a cure for trade depression requires statement under several heads.

First stands the widely accepted belief in 'the economy of high wages.' So far as it holds good, it rejects the primary assumption of wage-reduction viz. that it reduces costs of production, by asserting that such wage reduction will be attended by a more than corresponding fall in efficiency and productivity of labour. But 'the economy of high wages' has never been held to be of universal and unlimited application. Its strongest case has been against the definitely 'sweated' industries, whose wages have been inadequate to sustain the worker in effective health and physical strength. Relatively high wages and standards of consumption are admittedly necessary, in the physiological sense, to sustain the output of great and continuous muscular or nervous energy in hard and taxing occupations. Nor can conventional elements of class comfort and psychological factors of personal dignity and aspiration be ignored in exploring 'the economy of high wages.' But it will be urged with some force that this economy has definite limitations. It will generally be admitted that a sudden or rapid large increase in wage-rates is not normally accompanied at once by increased efficiency and productivity of labour. On the contrary, its early effect is often detrimental. The growing of new wholesome needs and satisfactions in a standard of living is often a slow process. Sudden new increments of income are seldom put to the best uses by any class of recipients. Hence a sudden considerable rise of wage-rates may and often does mean either that fewer days are worked, or that more money is spent in ways detrimental to efficiency, or at any rate in ways not conducive to higher efficiency. In process of time the higher wage-income may be assimilated in a better family standard of living, conducive to better health, higher intelligence, and generally improved efficiency.

But one of the most injurious effects of these trade fluctuations is that they unsettle standards of living and stop these gradual processes of improvement. Under such a dispensation, just as it cannot be assumed that wage-increases beyond the immediate limits of physiological efficiency will at once or quickly or of necessity be represented in higher productive efficiency, so it cannot be assumed that a reduction of these higher wages will be attended by a corresponding fall of efficiency and productivity. So far as immediate costs of production are concerned, there is much evidence to sustain the view that low-wage periods mean low labour-costs and high wage periods high labour-costs in trades where normal wage minima are above any 'sweating' level. If this view be correct, the 'economy of high wages' cannot be pleaded as a sufficient answer to the claim for wage-reduction, regarded from the standpoint of immediate trade policy.

The resistance of the workers to wage-reductions at such a time must be based upon a longer-sighted view of labour policy. A momentary view of the immediate situation may tempt them to accept a reduction, upon the plea that thus more employment can be found and the actual volume of wages can be raised. But the habitual adoption of this policy means that wage-increases, obtained in times of good trade, cannot be assimilated in a higher normal standard of living and thus cannot contribute to build up a higher standard of personal and economic efficiency for the working-class family. Once accept the principle that wage-rates must follow the fluctuations of prices and profits, instability of wages and of standards of living follow as a necessary consequence. Now this instability of standards is the worst count in labour's indictment of the 'capitalist system.' It is the chief gravamen of the charge that labour is treated as 'a commodity,' that is as a non-human factor of production. The demand that labour shall adapt itself in modes of life to industrial fluctuations over which it has very little control, accepting rises and falls of wages to correspond with these fluctuations, robs labour of the primary condition of progress in civilised life.

Yet this appears to be the policy urged by our business men and accepted by many of our economists, on the ground that a refusal on the part of labour defies the inevitable operation of economic laws.

It is just here that I would join issue both with the logic and the social utility of the policy. The laws which regulate prices, and through prices wages, are not inevitable in the sense that they operate by forces wholly external to the will and conduct of the workers. So long as labour in emergencies allows itself to be treated as a commodity in accepting wage reductions, employers will calculate upon such compliance and will make prices which take it into due account. That is to say, the habit of allowing wages to fall with falling prices is itself a cause of falling prices. If employers knew that wage-increases once obtained would be held, they might be slow to concede these increases, but they could not base future contracts upon lower wage-rates to be extorted or cajolled from trade unions hampered by heavy unemployment benefits. In other words, this insistence of labour on retaining a larger share of the product would be itself one important factor in controlling fluctuations of prices and trade. Thus a good deal of the otherwise 'inevitable' would be avoided.

Labour's firm stand for a rising standard of civilised life and the insistent retention of any improvement in that life would modify considerably the magnitude of the fluctuations hitherto made possible by the 'elasticity' of wages.

The history of 'sliding-scales' in wage agreements testifies to the influence of elasticity of wages in aggravating fluctuations of trade by enabling employers to gamble upon future wage reductions.

This wholesome general reaction upon the volume and regularity of trade follows from the adoption of our general analysis of trade depression. The acceptance of real wage reductions in bad times as inevitable and desirable means acceptance of the prevailing conditions of the distribution of wealth as between capital and labour, which we regard as the root cause of fluctuations and depressions. The refusal of such wage reduction makes for a more equal distribution of wealth, a better balance of production and consumption, and a fuller and more regular use of all factors of production.

The first answer, then, to those who urge that a real wage reduction in bad times will, by lowering costs of production, bring some recovery of trade and an increased aggregate income to the workers, is that this short-range expediency ignores the reaction of this compliant policy upon the distribution of the product which is the root cause of depression and unemployment. It can only win a temporary alleviation by sowing the seeds of future trouble. Under existing conditions a depression can only be worked out by a period of low production and low profits in which the reduced product is distributed favourably to labour, unfavourably to capital, so that the rate of saving is temporarily depressed and the insistence of consumers on retaining as much as possible of its normal rate of consumption gradually depletes the congested stocks which have choked the avenues of commerce and checked production.

The policy of wage reduction, raising the proportion of profits to wages, and reducing the proportion of consumption to production, will only lengthen the process of absorbing the congested stocks, in order that the whole movement may begin again.

Another reason for resisting wage reduction is that the adoption of this way of reducing costs of production has always operated to prevent the adoption of better ways. The assertion that high labour costs would ruin trade has been the stock argument of the industrialists against all the wage-advances, shortenings of hours, and legislation for the protection of employees, during the past hundred years. It has consistently been refuted by facts. High wages and other costs of labour have everywhere operated as incentives for employers to discover, adopt and improve other economies, technical and administrative, which have more than offset the higher cost of labour. The refusal of labour to accept reductions is a psychological condition of these other economies whose social and economic advantages are far greater. To lower costs of production by reducing wages is to take a backward step in civilisation: to achieve the same result by some improvement in machinery or process, some economy of the use of power, by discovering and developing a market for some by-product, by better book-keeping, cost taking, and management, is to take a forward step in civilisation. The former method, by degrading the standards of working-class life, not merely impedes the productivity of labour, but by breeding discontent makes it more difficult to introduce and operate successfully all technical and administrative reforms. The latter method operates immediately to increase the volume of output per unit of capital and labour employed, and harmonises high wages with high profits. My point here is that the better method will only be adopted if the worse is not available. In America it is generally recognised that the high wages obtainable by all skilled and much unskilled labour in industry operated as the potent stimulus to the great economies in mass production, mass-transport, and larger use of machines and mechanical power, which distinguish their industrial system. So long as Germany was a low-wage country of unorganised workers, her industrial development was low and slow. Only in the latter years of last century and the opening years of this did the socialist and trade-union organisation for higher wages and better labour conditions incite the great industrialists and organisers to apply to industry the superior scientific training and other qualities of brain and organisation by which they achieved pre-eminence in many lines of industry.

Employers clamour in a single breath for wage-cutting and for increased productivity. But wage-cutting does nothing for the real and lasting increase of productivity. It only serves to increase the product by employing more men at lower rates, reducing somewhat the efficiency per man. If, instead, employers are driven in times of depression to devise technical, administrative and financial economies, they secure real and lasting increases of productivity per unit of capital and labour employed. Labour, therefore, does not, as is sometimes contended, obstruct industrial recovery and progress by its refusal to accept wage reductions. On the contrary, by taking the determined position: "First exhaust all other economies before you touch wages," it applies a powerful stimulus to the discovery and adoption of every sort of technical and administrative improvement. The experience of Trade Boards shows how the fixing of standard wages in a trade compels the backward businesses to adopt the ways of working which prevail among the best-equipped businesses. The slovenly-minded employer in every trade is prone to assume the permanence of the *status quo.* He thinks he has proved his case for a wage-cut, as against a wage-rise, by showing that *under existing conditions* he cannot make a 'fair' or any profit. Thus the acceptance by labour of wage reductions as inevitable in bad trade offers a premium on managerial inefficiency and lack of enterprise. It is, moreover, an anti-social policy. For a business made profitable by low wages makes no real progress in productivity, whereas profits secured as the result of improved methods of production involve an increase of wealth and of attendant welfare.

It may, however, be said that labour in this country, as elsewhere, often offers an obstinate resistance to such improvements of technique and administration as are here suggested.

The difficulty on the part of labour arises from those conditions of distribution which, as we have seen, are responsible for restrictions of the market. Labour fears improvements because it fears that they signify displacement of workers and wage-cuts. Some employers in their greed for gain have sought to secure for themselves the profits of both economies—improved economies of production and lower wages. But these fears of improved productivity on the part of labour are scouted by most intelligent leaders. The modern labour policy is to encourage improvements in production and administration and to insist that a due proportion of the gains of these reforms shall come to the wage-earner. This more enlightened attitude is well expressed in the following statement from a document issued in 1919 by the American Federation of Labour:

> The question of increased productivity is not a question of putting upon the toilers a more severe strain; it is a question of vast fundamental changes in the management of industry, a question of the elimination of outworn policies; a question of the introduction of the very best in machinery and methods of management.

How enormous are these available economies in the single matter of the use of power has been brought out by several recent specialist Reports, showing the general neglect of employers in great industries like iron and steel to adopt known and proved economies of the generation and use of power. "It seems probable that if all the iron- and steel-works in this country adopted the most efficient methods, they could, on an average, improve their output by something between 50 and 100 per cent."[1] But the iron and steel trade will not perform this real economy if they can apply the easy, false, and socially injurious economy of wage reduction.

There is, however, a third reason why wage reduction in most industries serving home markets is a bad remedy for trade depression. In an economic order where trusts, combines and other associations for price-control exist, there is no security that wage-reduction will not simply be absorbed in higher profits, without leading to increased production and employment.

Experience of the last two years affords abundant testimony to the power of business combinations in the later stages of manufacture or of distribution to intercept and hold for themselves in higher margins of profit the falls in price of materials and labour in the earlier stages of production. The recent lag in the fall of many retail prices is quite evidently due to this power to divert to profits the economy of low wages and other costs of production. If wage-cuts produced at once corresponding cuts in retail

[1] *Industrial Fatigue Research Board Report* 5, p. 95.

prices, there would at any rate be some security for an immediate expansion of employment and consumption. But with so much of our industry in the clutches of strong combinations there is no safeguard for the interest either of the worker or of the consumer.

But, it may be urged, these arguments against wage reductions, especially the last, are only applicable in their full force to trades working for the home market. Now the most urgent demand for wage reductions is in our trades working for the world-market which find themselves undersold everywhere by the cheaper products of low-waged countries, especially Germany. It is just here that the present reality of 'the limited market' presses us severely. If the economic world went round as smoothly as theorists imagined, and consumption was ready and able at once to take everything that could be produced, there would be no plausibility in the demand that we must cut our wages, because we have forced German wages down to a level on which she can virtually undersell us in all foreign markets. Given a fully effective world-market, there would be nothing to prevent us producing goods for that market on a higher level of wages than that of Germany. We should not produce exactly the same lines of goods, for Germany would specialise in those lines where her cheaper labour gave her the largest margin of gain. We should undertake lines of production and trade in which, though Germany could undersell us if she undertook them, she would not compete because her capital and labour would be more profitably absorbed in the lines where her advantages were greater. Such is the well-known theory of international trade, operating by division of labour and specialisation. Unfortunately it does not apply where the world-market is so restricted as it is now. For in the trough of such a world depression as prevails at present, the world market for most materials and manufactures has shrunk so much that a single big industrial nation, such as Germany, could absorb so much of it, as to leave very little for countries working at definitely higher costs of production. Where two countries depend so much for the subsistence and employment of their peoples upon the same lines of export trade as Britain and Germany, the issue stands out very sharply. It not only appears to be, but is, to the immediate interest of British trade, and even of the British workers, to lower their standard of wages towards that of the German workers, in order to obtain thereby a larger share of the restricted world-market. It is not a sufficient reply, as we have seen, to urge that lower wages will reduce the internal demand for our products; for that objection is met by showing that an increased volume of employment will mean a larger aggregate of income though the individual worker's income may be less. Nor is the plea for reduction disposed of by urging that the present gap between real wages here and in Germany is so wide that no wage-cuts contemplated here will reduce costs of production near to the German level. For, granted that the general labour costs in Germany are much lower than here, it by no means follows that considerable wage-cuts here would not enable us to get contracts which would otherwise go to Germany, provided that our prices can approach near the German prices. For over that large section of the world-market under the flag of the Allied Powers there remains a strong sentimental preference for our goods over those of Germany, which can be 'cashed' in selling prices, provided that the preference is such as the purchasers think they can afford. Moreover, even under existing conditions there are certain lines of production where our hold upon the market has been too strong to be displaced by cheaper German goods. Finally, the production of more export goods, competing with those of Germany, will, by increasing the total supply, reduce the selling prices still further, and by stimulating effective demand in the foreign markets which have hitherto been depressed, will restore a higher total quantity of export trade beyond the limits of Germany's capacity to supply. Thus, it would appear temporarily advantageous to lower our wages towards the German level.

This is the supreme temptation which every period of trade depression presents to the peoples with higher standards of living, an immediate gain in markets and employment if they will lower these standards towards the level of those other countries which have been able to get the lion's share of the depressed and restricted world-market because of the cheapness of production. The present case is only an extreme example of the position which recurs in every general cyclical depression. It has been exaggerated by the circumstances of the War, and especially by the pressure upon Germany for reparations, which forces her continually to inflate her currency and so secretly to reduce the real wages and costs of production in her industries. The folly of this operation is now generally recognised. But it is proper to dwell not upon the special features of the present case, but upon the fact that the problem of the immediate utility of wage reductions belongs to the general problem of cyclical depressions.

It is the greatest single peril to the progress of the working-classes in the higher-waged industrial countries. In periods of trade depression and restricted world-markets it may appear to peoples in these developed countries better to take lower wages than to support large bodies of unemployed workers out of currently reduced resources, just as we have seen that in these same conditions it appears advantageous to keep out by protective tariffs cheaper foreign goods that seek to enter our home markets and enlarge our unemployment. In fact, these two policies of lower wages and protective tariffs are partly complementary and partly alternative remedies against the disease of trade depressions. By keeping out foreign goods entering our markets at prices lower than those at which we can produce, we may relieve ourselves from the necessity of lowering our wages to meet this competition. This, of course, is the familiar and plausible plea for working-class support for protection, which has a short range efficacy similar to that appertaining to the policy of wage reduction. By lowering wages we enable our home trades immediately to expand (with the qualifications recognised above) and improve our export trade by securing an increased proportion of the restricted market. But our industrialists, though they might prefer to couple their demand for tariffs with a demand for lower wages, would probably be willing to surrender the latter demand, if it seemed politically necessary in order to win the suffrages of workers for their tariff by representing it as the shield of a high-wage system.

This exploration of the policy of wage-reduction in times of trade depression serves to bring out two extremely critical positions. The first is the continual danger to which higher standards of wages and living are exposed by the recurrence of these periods of depression and restricted markets. This danger is greatest for those advanced nations which are most dependent for foods and raw materials upon foreign countries and which must find foreign markets for their manufactures in order to purchase these essentials. Great Britain, Germany and Italy, among the great powers, are most exposed to these dangers, and the War has greatly increased their dependence upon foreign markets, by enlarging their foreign indebtedness and reducing their foreign investments. For us, with our dependence on overseas supplies for half our food, it is of literally vital importance to meet this danger of recurrent attacks upon our standard of wages and living in the only way in which it can be met, namely by international co-operation for the maintenance of standards of work and life for labour.

Economic internationalism of a constructive order, supported by the necessary intergovernmental apparatus, is the essential instrument for the maintenance of the industry and standard of life of our people.

We cannot, as could the United States, Russia, or France, maintain our economic civilisation out of our own national resources, with such slight external commerce as would always be available. We must continue to work for a world-market and to buy and sell in that market more largely than ever as a condition of economic survival and progress. Now in this world-market at any given time there can only be one price for any supply of goods or services. If our manufactures or trades hold a practical monopoly in certain export lines, no difficulty connected with labour standards need arise. But where, as is commonly the case, our goods compete directly or indirectly with similar goods produced in other countries whose powers of production are expanding, we are liable to be ousted from these markets by manufacturers in other countries whose lower costs of production enable them to quote lower prices. This displacement will occur chiefly at periods of trade depression when restricted markets favour buyers. So far, therefore, as lower wages are consistent with efficient or genuinely cheap production, each recurring period of depression must be reflected in a higher rate of unemployment in the high-waged countries than in the low-waged. Since England is the high-waged country most dependent upon foreign markets, she is most exposed to this damage.

She has a double interest in an international policy for raising the standards of labour. By assisting to secure minimum standards of wages, hours, and other conditions for labour in backward industrial countries, she adopts the only effective means of safeguarding her export trade against the assaults of sweated industries in these backward countries, in times of slack or depressed trade, when there is not enough market to go round. This policy does not involve the adoption by all the competing countries of identical or even closely approximate standards of wages or hours. It is not necessary to insist that Indian or Chinese labour should be paid the same rates as prevail in Lancashire. But what is necessary is that any rise in wages or other labour costs obtained in Lancashire shall be accompanied by some fairly corresponding rise in wages or other conditions in India, China and other competing countries, and that in periods of world-depression wage-cuts shall not be arbitrarily made in other countries so as to enable their manufactures to displace ours. Unless some such policy, difficult as it may be to operate, can be adopted, there can be no security for employment and wage standards for our workers in export trades, and the low standards and insecurity in these export trades must react in an injurious way upon our home industries.

For though the pressure of high labour costs in stimulating other technical and administrative economies of production *may* enable certain of our trades to hold their own in competing with cheaper labour in foreign countries, there is no adequate safeguard here against the competition of highly developed countries like Germany and America, where high technical and administrative efficiency may be conjoined with a more flexible wage system, or where extremely cheap labour may be employed in producing inferior qualities of goods which may oust our superior qualities in periods of world impoverishment.

If we are to retain within our national area the volume of trade and employment needed to maintain our growing population upon a rising standard of life, we must come to some definite arrangements with other countries supplying the world-market to march along the same road of economic progress at something like the same pace. Unless we do this, an ever stronger tendency will operate to draw industries from this country and place them in countries where the net costs of production are lower.

It is a continuation of the same process which during our Industrial Revolution drew our scattered textile and other manufactures from rural districts into large towns situated near the new sources of power, or which now are beginning to decentralise some of these same industries so as to avail themselves of the cheaper land and labour of our villages. If it be found feasible to produce standard manufactures more cheaply in Russia, China or Japan, having regard to the joint economy of improved machine production and cheap labour, it seems inevitable that a good deal of our past industry will leave England and pass into these cheaper areas of production.

There may be some who will regard this process of transfer as not merely inevitable but desirable. Others may feel regret or even dismay at such a prospect, but still be sceptical about the feasibility of any economic internationalism competent to check it. But it is at any rate of vital importance that the disturbing prospect should be realised, and that friends of British labour should bestir themselves to try what international co-operation can do to mitigate the disturbance, and, if possible, to stop the sweated labour in foreign countries from underselling us in the world-market. The International Labour Bureau, attached to the League of Nations, is at any rate the possible instrument of such a co-operative policy, though its present feebleness is attested by the contemptuous treatment accorded by most governments to its early conventions.

So far I have treated this international co-operation from the exclusively British standpoint as a means of preventing the degradation of our wages in periods ot trade depression. But there is a wider and more fundamental significance attaching to international co-operation for the maintenance and improvement of the standards of labour in all countries by consent. For this is the only safe way in which the world-product can be distributed more equally and equitably between labour and the other claimants. The better distribution within a single national area, such as Britain, would not secure its object. It might drive a good deal of the trade, capital and labour, to other national areas where profits were higher and wages lower. It is literally true that for a country in close dependence upon other countries, as is ours, no single problem of trade or labour can be solved upon a purely national basis. A common international policy is the only way of remedying that fundamental maladjustment between rate of production and rate of consumption, of which trade depressions and the ills they bring are at once the evidence and the consequence. Any effective internationalism which should operate throughout the industrial world to put a larger share of the product in the possession of the workers, and to reduce the existing inequality of incomes in the various classes, would not merely help the advanced countries to hold their own, but would strike directly at the origin of the cyclical fluctuations and depressions. For such an improvement in the general distribution of wealth would, as we have seen, signify a stronger and more continuous demand for consumable goods, with the result that the factors of production would be kept fully employed. In presenting the general argument in the foregoing chapters, I purposely refrained from raising the question how far it was capable of successful application within a single national area. The issue has frequently been raised in the case of certain low grade branches of the clothing trades and other definitely sweated industries. Two lines are frequently taken. The first is to insist upon the abolition of sweating conditions, with the object of levelling up the bad businesses to the level of the good ones, under the conviction that they can by such compulsion be made to pay their way on improved conditions of labour. This, the policy of the early Trade Boards, has been generally successful. Parasitic businesses have been converted into self-supporting ones, wage standards have been raised and improved methods of work have been maintained. But it is admitted that there are cases where sweating is necessary to make a business pay. The accepted social policy in such a case is that a civilised country cannot afford to keep within its borders businesses which are degrading the labour they employ, and poisoning the industrial system upon which they are parasitic. We had better do without trades that can only survive in these low conditions.

This is, no doubt, a sound social position to take. But it is idle to deny that it might be a costly one, where the cases in question were not minor branches of domestic trades but large national industries If there is a risk of the standards of wages and other costs of labour in our staple export manufactures being challenged successfully by the competition of cheap labour countries in the world-market whenever trade collapses, the only real remedy against the woeful dilemma of unemployment or low wages thus prescribed is a strengthening of the world-demand which prevents trade from collapsing. Only by regarding the industrial world as a single economic system, and treating it as such, can the problem of under-consumption and unemployment be tackled with success. To regard the national industry of such a country as ours, or, indeed, that of any advanced country, as a separate area of economic settlement is evidently an illusion. Economic peace and progress can only be attained by common rules of international conduct contributory to a more equal and more equitable apportionment of work and its product over the whole area of the world-market. However slow and difficult the road to this goal may be, it is the only road, and the sooner it is surveyed and opened for the common use of nations the better for the civilisation of the world.

CHAPTER VII

CREDIT AS A FACTOR IN FLUCTUATIONS

A WIDER aspect of the credit question remains for consideration in connection with the present and prospective situation. The use of abundant bank credits during a trade expansion operates, as we recognise, favourably to profits, unfavourably to wages, owing to the wage-lag. During a trade depression the balance is temporarily redressed, at any rate in part, wages and subsidies for unemployment forming a larger proportion of the reduced current real income than in normal times. But since the operations of credit admittedly serve to exaggerate the fluctuations of prices and of trade, they afford increased opportunities to make gains out of speculation and manipulation of the money and the produce-markets. As the ordinary business man becomes more dependent upon bank asistance, alike for doing profitable trade in good times and for holding on in bad times, bankers, and other manufacturers of credit, are in a position to take a heavier toll from industry and commerce. Though it is easy to exaggerate the share of the general income which thus passes to the controllers of finance, its growing size is a factor in the problem of distribution. But the operation of credit serving, as we saw, to swell profits of business men in times of good trade, has during the last few years exercised a larger and more enduring influence upon the distribution of income. For during that period the necessities of government in every belligerent and most neutral state led to the creation of vast quantities of credits, issued either directly by governments as uncovered and inconvertible currency notes, or by banks as advances to governments or private customers, for a purpose wholly different from the commercial purposes of ordinary bank credits. The latter, as we see, help in ordinary times to stimulate production by applying more purchasing power to the employment of unused factors of production, or to the better grouping and intensive utilisation of factors already employed. Although the first immediate effect of issuing such credit is to raise prices, this effect is counteracted so soon as its secondary effect in stimulating production has been attained. So far as bank credit enables more goods to be produced, or, what is the same thing, to move with greater rapidity and facility through the economic system, it does not raise prices and is not 'inflation.'

There are, however, conditions under which bank credit does act as inflation. Where, as during the latter half of the war, the full resources of the country were already fully mobilised for production, further bank credits could not perform this stimulative work. They could at most enable the businesses which received them to secure a larger share of the more lucrative contracts than other businesses, i.e they gave a merely competitive advantage without producing any appreciable net economy. This applies to ordinary periods of trade revival or prosperity where excessive confidence leads traders and bankers to expect and provide for further advances of trade, prices and profits, which are not going to take place.

These misuses, or excesses, of commercial credit are responsible for exaggerating the cyclical fluctuations, but they do not have any considerable effect upon the permanent distribution of wealth as between the different classes. For the greater part of the large profits made in the rising prices and expanding trade of a boom is lost in the subsequent depression.

But the war-period exhibited credit phenomena which have left lasting results of a different kind. A large part of the war credit, created either by governments or banks for financing the war, did very little to stimulate the total volume of production. It operated to convert a larger and larger proportion of the same volume of production into war supplies, a smaller proportion into civil supplies. Thus, increasing the volume of purchasing power without any corresponding increase of output, it was pure inflation, and was responsible for the great rise of prices that ensued. In proportion as various countries financed their national expenditure by these means, they were preparing a huge debt which was to alter the subsequent distribution of the national income to the advantage of the 'capitalist' classes and the disadvantage of the workers, entailing those reactions upon regularity and fullness of employment which we have already discovered. The connection between the inflation which the governments and banks conspired to produce and the magnitude and ownership of the war debts is not obscure. The 'money' which the governments got by printing notes, by borrowing from banks, or by inciting banks to give credit to customers in order to increase subscriptions to war loans (all pure inflation), they spent in buying goods and services. Thus prices and profits mounted up the faster, because this easy way of getting money made governments more careless in the rates they paid for what they bought. The immense and rapid profits —due to the expanding prices, with a lag of wages and a virtual elimination of competition—the recipients invested in war-loans, the only authorised and available investment. At the end of the war, in this country, the bond-holding class had established, by savings from these inflated war profits, a claim to deduct for the annual income of the people of this country, a sum of nearly £400 millions.[1] With booming trade and high prices, this sum probably represented about 10 per cent. of the national income. With declining trade, falling prices and falling income, this fixed sum signifies an increasing percentage. If our national income fell to its pre-war level, the burden of war-interest would amount to between 15 per cent. and 20 per cent. of the total income. Now this burden differs from every other form of 'unearned income' in that, whereas rent, interest and profits are paid to the owners of some factor of production whose current productive use contributes to the increase of the real income of the country, no such claim can be made for the ownership of war

[1] The interest on floating debt is here added to the annual interest on War Loans.

debt. There is no current source out of which the payment of this interest can be made, except the incomes of other members of the community. Now, if the war debt were held by all classes in some approximate proportion to their incomes, this might not matter. But, as we have seen, war conditions enabled the war profiteers to supply the vast majority of the loans. Of the £7,400 millions held here in State securities in 1920, only £567 millions were held by 'small investors,' and of these a large proportion would not be workers. The hard times of last year again have greatly reduced the amount held by small investors. At the end of the depression virtually the whole of the debt will be held by the well-to-do classes, forming a considerable reduction in the proportion of the current income of the nation available as purchasing power for the working classes. If this is the result of our war finance, it applies far more severely to most other belligerent countries, whose war expenditure was defrayed far more largely out of inflation, unless the permanent adoption of lower monetary values effects a proportionate cancelment of debt.

War finance in a word, it would thus appear, has considerably aggravated the maldistribution of income which is the source of trade fluctuations, unemployment, and the political and economic maladies which flow from these conditions. But in Great Britain, as in most other modern states, progressive methods of direct taxation of incomes and inheritances go far to redress the balance. The increasing proportion of tax revenue, taken from the higher unearned incomes and the larger estates, for the service of war debts, pensions, and other obligations, has probably absorbed in this country, as in Germany, Italy and the United States, most of the contribution which interest on war loans makes to the incomes of the well-to-do. Only in countries, such as France, where direct progressive taxation is notably inadequate and where the indirect taxes are largely borne by working class consumers, is there reason to conclude that the net result of war finance has been a worsening of the relative condition of the workers.

But there are other changes of class incomes—partly due to the war, partly to more general causes—which should be taken into account in considering how far tendencies favour a more equal distribution of income and a consequently improved adjustment between production and consumption. The damage inflicted upon the professional and salaried classes in most countries has been strongly marked. This has been partly due to weak organisation and personal ineptitude for bargaining, but chiefly to a numerical over-supply at a time when large bodies of consumers found it necessary to economise upon their less urgent needs, and many business firms to cut down their salariat. Large sections of the professional and employed middle classes have been reduced to poverty and want in Austria, Germany and other broken countries; and elsewhere, as in Great Britain, have suffered great damage to their economic status. Not entirely a war change, this dwindling of the economic strength of the rank and file of the brain-workers has been greatly accelerated by the war.

With any strong economic revival some improvement in their condition may be expected. But the spread of educational opportunities must definitely weaken their position as claimants for income. Always a saving class, their contribution to the general investment fund will be diminished.

Set on the other hand a remarkable strengthening of the economic position of farmers and agriculturists in every country. Here, again, the war has accelerated a tendency visible before, viz. a relative shortage of the world supply of staple foods and raw materials and a consequent rise of prices. War profits made by these classes in all countries, belligerent or neutral, were immense, and in few cases was any successful attempt made by governments to secure an adequate contribution to the war or post-war taxation. This failure to impose taxation upon recent increments of land values and agricultural incomes, is largely responsible for the excessive taxes which in some countries are crippling industrial enterprise. Here is an aspect of the important economic and political cleavage between town and country. The large savings made in recent years by this notoriously thrifty class passed largely into the possession of landlords, where tenants used their profits to purchase their farms or where landlords were free to raise their rents. But in countries where peasant ownership prevailed, these gains were largely invested in war loans and other public securities, and involved an important change in the balance of class power in national policy, especially on matters of taxation and finance.

Thirdly, a certain levelling up of wages as between

skilled and unskilled, manual and non-manual labour, is visible in most countries. During the war, when money and real wages were rising, the lower male grades rose proportionately more than the higher, women more than men, children and young persons more than adults. After the war, when conditions became more normal, some of this change has been maintained. On the whole, in this and other countries, the fall of skilled wage-rates during the depression has been greater than that of unskilled wage-rates. If, as is likely, this tendential equalisation of wage-rates continues to operate, it will have some effect in introducing a new saving habit into larger grades of the workers, whose former earnings left no margin for saving over their necessary or conventional standard of living. But so small is the proportion of the working class contribution as a whole to the new capital fund that for our particular problem this change is not significant. It is doubtful whether any change, which does not bring a considerable improvement both of real income and security to the workers as a whole, will appreciably increase the proportion of their contribution to the saving fund, and only if that improvement was obtained largely at the expense of the capitalist and other wealthy classes, would it make appreciably for an improved adjustment between spending and saving, production and consumption.

The other alterations in the relative condition of the professional and salaried middle classes and the agriculturists may fairly be held to cancel out in most industrially developed countries, where town life is relatively strong. Only in countries predominantly rural in their character does the new situation make perceptibly for a growing proportion of saving to spending. For the rural populations are at once more conservative in the standard of living, and are put in possession of larger surpluses for saving.

In developed industrial countries the attainment of a better distribution of income, in order to secure a better adjustment between production and consumption, depends upon whether the wage-earners and the State can between them absorb most of the unearned and unneeded surplus of the rich. So far as the struggle is a purely economic one between organised labour and organised capital, it is not easy to see how the former can prevail, unless it can both obtain a normal basic wage which leaves little surplus profit and also stop the wage-lag which, assisted by speculative credit, is seen to be responsible for over-production and consequent depression. During a depression the power of organised capital to break down the wage standards and bring labour to heel, is implicit in the economic situation. Labour can only defend itself effectively by political weapons, supposing it can get them and learn how to use them.

In this truly political economy there are three chief instruments. The first is the establishment of a common rule of minimum conditions of labour and of living, in the shape of wage, hour and other conditions, made obligatory in all employments. The second is the assumption by the State, municipality or other governing body, of the ownership and operation of (or at least the control of wages, prices and other conditions in) those essential services and industries which, left to private enterprise, exhibit a strongly monopolistic character. The third is the scientific application of the State powers of taxation, so as to secure for public consumption as much as possible of those surplus earnings that accrue from lucrative businesses which it is convenient to leave to private enterprise.

Here, of course, I merely cite the three familiar departments of progressive economy. But though they seem at first sight only to aim at improved distribution of income, if our analysis of the situation be correct, this progressive economy must be equally effective for the stimulation of enlarged production; for our starting point was the recognition of the huge waste of productive power in our present economic system, attested by the habitual under-use of most of our productive factors, the misapplication of much of them in purely wasteful competition and the periodic idleness of a large part of them.

This actual waste, far exceeding any accepted measurement of unemployment, we traced to the operations in the economic system of a great body of surplus income representing maldistribution. Thus we recognise the problem of greater productivity to be, in fact, inseparable from that of better distribution.

There are those who hold that the solution of this problem can only be achieved by a destruction of the entire fabric of 'the capitalist system.' For only thus, they hold, can the 'surplus income' which causes our maladies be properly absorbed. If they can show that some such wholesale revolution of our economic arrangements is politically feasible, and that their new system will satisfy the needs of high productivity as well as of equitable distribution, they are right to go behind the progressive policy here cited. I am satisfied to leave the proposals for reform at a point that is in line with the actual movements which I perceive to be in operation in most modern industrial communities, disbelieving both in the need and the practicability of wholesale sudden transformations, either in human nature or the institutions it imposes.

CHAPTER VIII

THE DOUGLAS THEORY

It was inevitable that at a time like this, when the disturbances of financial machinery are so grave and so widespread, there should spring up schools of thought which find in the defects of our credit system a complete explanation of the industrial collapse. The most noteworthy of these schools is founded on the writings of Major Douglas. With a part of his diagnosis of the present trouble I find myself in cordial agreement. I agree with him in attributing trade depression to the failure of consumption, or effective demand, to keep pace with potential and actual production. The full product cannot be produced because, if produced, it could not be marketed at the price required under our actual system to make production profitable.

But Major Douglas and his followers give a different explanation of the failure of this effective demand from that which I should give. I trace this failure, not to any lack of the monetary power to purchase all the commodities that could be produced, but to the refusal of those in possession of this power of purchase to apply enough of it in buying consumables, because they prefer to apply it to buying non-consumables, in other words, to buying capital goods.

According to the Douglas theory, however, as I understand it, it is economically impossible for all the commodities that could be produced to get sold, because the income to buy them all does not exist. Indeed, it goes still further, by insisting not merely that potential production is curbed by this deficiency of purchasing power, but that the market for part of the actual products is deficient for the same cause.

The least unintelligible summary of the doctrine in Major Douglas's own writings runs as follows [1]:

1. Price cannot normally be less than cost plus profit.
2. Cost includes all expenditure on product.
3. Therefore cost involves all expenditure on consumption (food, clothes, housing, etc.) paid for out of the wages, salaries or dividends, as well as all expenditure on factory account, also representing previous consumption.
4. Since it includes this expenditure, the portion of the cost represented by this expenditure has already been paid by the recipients of wages, salaries and dividends.
5. These represent the community; therefore the only distribution of real purchasing power in respect of production over a unit period of time is the surplus wages, salaries and dividends available after all subsistence, expenditure and cost of materials consumed has been deducted. The surplus production, however, includes all this expenditure in cost, and consequently in price.
6. The only effective demand of the consumer, therefore, is a few per cent. of the price value of commodities, and is cash credit. The remainder of the home effective demand is loan credit, which is controlled by the banker, the financier, and the industrialist, in the interest of production with a financial objective, not in the interest of the ultimate consumer.

Now here the central charge is that only a small fraction of the money representing costs of production

[1] *Economic Democracy*, pp. 70–71.

and gathered into sale-price is available for purchasing goods, and it is implied, though not explicitly stated, that no other sufficient power of purchase is available. Costs are, it appears, not available as purchase money for two widely different reasons. The money represented in wages, salaries and dividends, paid to the producers of these goods for producing them, have for the most part been spent already by their recipients in purchases for current consumption, before the goods, into whose costs they entered, had reached the retail stores. Only such small fraction of these 'costs,' as has been withheld from current expenditure, is available for purchase of these goods.

The other sort of 'costs,' viz. expenditure on factory account, overhead charges, purchase of raw materials, etc., is not available for another reason. It represents bank credit, advances made by bankers to manufacturers and merchants out of a body of banking credit available only for this work of financing trade, and not for the ultimate purchase of the goods produced. Thus, Major Douglas reaches his conclusion that "the only effective demand of the consumer is a few per cent. of the price-value of commodities."

Now the first and most obvious comment on this analysis is that it proves too much. If it were true that only "a few per cent." of the cost were available for purchase, the entire economic system must speedily be brought almost to a standstill. The recent 20 per cent. of industrial unemployment would be a trifle compared with the situation here envisaged.

But it is quite evident that the effective demand of consumers is not confined to the unspent portion of the money producers have received for producing these particular goods. In the very propositions setting out his case, Major Douglas exposes the nature of his error, for he gives as the reason why the bulk of wages, salaries and dividends are not available for purchasing the final goods that they have already been spent upon goods previously produced. And this, of course, is the habitual course of trade. The money available for bringing the commodities which each week flow into the retail stores, to replace those sold last week, is not the money paid for producing these commodities, but that paid for the various processes just performed for producing the commodities that will reach the retail stores next week or next month. Effective demand for commodities proceeds from the wages, salaries and dividends quite recently paid to the producers of these commodities for making their successors. Unless a slump in trade, prices and employment, has intervened (which is not Major Douglas' contention), there is, therefore, no reason why the effective demand of consumers should be insufficient to purchase all the goods produced at a price covering all their costs of production.

But what about the costs which are incurred, not as wages, salaries, and dividends, but "on factory account, overhead charges, purchase of raw materials, etc."? These elements in the final prices are not, it is contended, available as effective demand for those commodities or for any other! Why not? What is the difference between the availability for purchasing commodities of the wages paid to workers in a shoe factory and those paid in a factory for making shoe machinery, to replace the machines gradually worn out in the shoe factory? So with all the other money paid in overhead charges, raw material, etc. There is no difference in the availability of these costs and the other costs, as effective demand for commodities.

Misunderstanding sometimes arises from the tendency to visualise productive effort as directed to three ends, the production of commodities, work of repair and replacement of capital goods, production of more capital goods. Now when production is properly realised, not as a single act or set of acts, but as a continuous process, the second of these ends (repair and replacement) simply disappears, i.e. is swallowed up in production of commodities, and the payments made on its behalf are available as effective demand for commodities, though not of the particular series of commodities into which they entered as costs.

Perhaps this is best realised by visualising production as a constant rapid flow of raw materials from the extractive processes of agriculture, mining, etc., through various stages of transport, manufacture and distribution, assisted at the several stages by plant, fuel and other capital goods which flow as tributaries into the main stream, being worked up into the final commodities and forming costs of production on a par with the other costs, wages, salaries and interest, in the main flow of production. The net income of the commodity will consist of wages, salaries and interest paid in all these productive processes, whether conducted on the main stream or along the tributaries. All this income is available for effective demand of commodities. Sometimes it is so applied; but in that case no saving, or creation of new capital goods, takes place. Normally, however, some of the net income paid to producers for productive effort is not expended upon consumable commodities, but upon the purchase of new capital goods (i.e. it is saved and invested). But this does not in the least imply that some of the commodities produced cannot get purchased, because the money which might have bought them has been saved. So far as this saving is a normal, calculable process, it means that part of the productive process will be devoted, not to making consumable goods, but to making more capital goods that will be purchased and owned by the savers.

That income which is saved is spent in buying (i.e. paying people to make) a larger quantity of capital goods, materials, semi-manufactured goods, machines, fuel, etc., with a view to turning out an increased quantity of commodities at some future time.

I hold that the trouble comes from an under-consumption, or an over-saving, an attempt to save and utilise for future production a larger proportion of the aggregate income than can be saved and utilised. This disproportion between saving and spending I attribute to the unequal distribution of income, which leads to a large amount of automatic accumulation and investment of unearned and excessive wealth. The futile attempt of these idle savings to find a remunerative use in the economic system clogs that system and congests it, causing those periodic gluts and stoppages which economists disguise or decorate under the title 'cyclical depressions.'

But this is a very different explanation from that adopted by Major Douglas.

But to treat the Douglas theory without any reference to bank credit would be to leave Hamlet out of the play. For it often appears as if the main source of trouble lay in the fact that bankers had to receive from the sale of goods the advances which they made to finance their production, and that, as these sums were not available for purchasing the goods, there was a huge deficiency of consuming power. Bank credits are advanced to business men at various stages of production and are used by them to pay wages, salaries, etc., and to purchase raw materials and machinery. Are not these payments costs of production? "If these have not gone into costs, where have they gone?" says Major Douglas.[1]

My answer is that if by 'these' be meant *the advances* made by the banks for financing productive operations, they do not go into costs. Only the price paid by the manufacturer or merchant to the banker for these advances goes into costs, i.e. the interest on the bank advance. I grant that if a particular business transaction, a single bank advance, be artificially severed from the continuous process to which it belongs, it may be made to appear that, as the manufacturer must repay this loan out of the only available fund, viz. the money paid him by the merchant for the goods, this money must be got out of the sale price of the goods, so figuring as a cost of their production. But business is not conducted in this way. The manufacturer engaged in

[1] *Socialist Review*, March 1922.

a line of business is not required to, and does not, repay the banker the sum of his advance out of the money he receives for the goods. He only pays the interest. The banker makes a continuous advance of a certain amount, receiving periodically from his client the price of this advance. Out of this interest, the banker pays wages, salaries and dividend in the banking business. These incomes, distributed in the banking business, are precisely on a par with the other incomes which figure in the factory, warehouse or shop as costs of production, and are available precisely in the same way as purchasing power to buy the goods produced.

This represents the normal play of industry and of finance. If it were true that the body of the bank advance formed a cost of production, and had to be repaid out of the prices received for the goods, the whole trade would stop with a jerk. Something like this actually happens when bankers get frightened and call in their money, refusing further advances. Here is the element of truth in the criticism of trade financing by banks. They wield a dangerous power of stopping suddenly what has grown to be a normal and a necessary method of conducting business. The result of this abnormal action of banks in calling in and constricting credit is to stop trade and cause unemployment and under-production. Such a result may, if we like, be said to be due to the necessity under which traders are placed of repaying bank advances out of the proceeds of their sales, diverting to this purpose the money which normally they could and would have used to pay wages, salaries, etc., for producing more goods. Under such abnormal circumstances alone can it be represented that the body of a bank loan, not the interest, forms a cost of production. It is not true of the normal play of manufacture and commerce

CHAPTER IX

REPLIES TO CRITICISM

I

In concluding my argument I think it is desirable to give a fuller and more formal reply to two lines of criticism which are likely to block its reception in many minds.

It may be said that this is a most inopportune time to press the claim of a doctrine of under-consumption or over-saving. The present depression and unemployment require and admit no such explanation. They are manifestly due to the destruction of capital resources and of the productive power of labour from the war and the social disorders which ensued in Central Europe, Russia and the near East, the breakdown of the financial system by which commerce between nations, and even within the several countries, is normally conducted, deficiencies in the machinery of transport, protective tariffs, embargoes and other obstacles to trade, the cost and difficulty of getting the fabric of industry from a war-basis on to a peace-basis, political insecurity and related wastes of armaments, high taxation, war debts, reparations, and the aggregate result of all these conditions in paralysing business confidence and the plans and activities which require a reliable monetary system. In the presence of these patent sources of depression, it may be said, why summon a large essentially speculative explanation which, even if applicable to ordinary cyclical depressions, cannot here apply ?

Indeed, to allude to under-consumption and over-saving as lying at the roots of our present situation may well seem the height of ineptitude. For is it not evident, I shall be told, that over-spending, the extravagance of Governments and private persons, the refusal to recognise that the damage and waste of war could only be repaired by a long spell of low living and hard work, and general thrift, are everywhere the causes of the failure of the world to make a good recovery ?

Now that the War and after-war phenomena just cited are proximate causes of depression is incontrovertible. They have given special shape to the cyclical depression otherwise due, and have exaggerated its dimensions. To the under-production and under-consumption of a normal depression they have added an under-production and under-consumption from the broken industries of devastated areas, from the depleted stocks and transport instruments in many undevastated areas and from the loss of customary markets for the goods they were capable of producing. But when it is contended that this trouble was an inevitable economic consequence ot the War, the meaning of this term 'inevitable' should be plainly realised. Great wars have commonly been followed by spells of poverty and depression, and shallow criticism contents itself with alleging that the great destruction of war can only be paid for in this way.

Now though there is an element of moral or psychological truth in this, it is not, strictly speaking, economically true. This world-war, destructive as it was, did not leave the world, as a whole, seriously diminished in its economic resources. It did not, even in Europe taken as a whole, so seriously reduce our productive resources as to make a long spell of poverty and recoupment inevitable. Almost all the economic cost of the War was defrayed out of the current real income of the world. For the actual destruction of buildings, roads, ships, factories, mines, farms, made a small proportion of the real cost of the War. The rest consisted of quantities of war supplies, including munitions, transport services, food, clothing, etc. representing the current production of the world during the years of war. Even the human cost, in the sense of loss of life and limb, was compensated from the economic standpoint by the normal growth of population in the economic world and, so far as Europe was concerned, in the stoppage of migration to the newer countries. Certain belligerent nations sustained large capital losses, by disposing of foreign investments and incurring foreign debts But this, of course, meant no diminution of the capital of the industrial world as a whole. Apart from the destruction of the War itself, and some letting down of stocks of raw materials and foodstuffs, quickly recoverable, the productive power of the world was not sensibly diminished by the War, except in the sense that the additions made to the capital fabric and to the labour-power were much smaller than they would have been had not four years of war reduced the rate of real saving and of the growth of population.

My point is that the direct economic damages of war did not leave the productive resources of the world so reduced as to render economically necessary the collapse which has taken place. It is true that over large areas of continental Europe supplies of raw materials, foods, fuel, transport and agricultural tools were lacking. But the world-supplies of most of these articles were abundant, and where there was a temporary shortage, as in coal and shipping, it was soon made up by the activity of the post-war period, nearly to the pre-war level.

Had a good peace been made, with a restoration of free commercial intercourse between nations, an emergency scheme of international credit to assist the recovery of the broken nations, a reduction of armaments and a stoppage of inflation, there seems no reason for supposing that the economic ravages of war might not have been speedily repaired, so that the pre-war production might have been resumed or even enlarged. We are only too well acquainted with the coil of political and economic crimes and follies which stopped this recovery. Minor wars, social disorders, blockades, tariffs and embargoes, armaments, reparations, extravagant budgets, inflation, fluctuating exchanges, crushing taxation, low productivity of labour—have all contributed to bring about this unprecedented depression of production and consumption, in which industrial activity is only found in a large enforced sweating system for countries with degraded currencies and low exchange whose cheapened exports tend to absorb the restricted world-market.

Now while it would be absurd to press a purely economic interpretation upon this piece of history, converting the fears, hatreds, ambitions and follies that it exhibits into terms of economic greed and error, close observers and analysts of the Peace Treaties and the whole post-war policy generally agree that economic considerations relating to possession of coal and iron, oil, and the control of undeveloped economic resources, and the routes of access to them, were determinant factors in those decisions which have so much aggravated our present troubles. In a word, the badness of the Peace and post-war policy is mainly the badness of an Imperialism whose tap-root lies in a struggle for markets and for the areas of lucrative investment of surplus savings derived from profitable business enterprises in the highly developed industrial countries The struggle of rival national Imperialisms has assumed an intensity and a variety of directions due to the political collapse of three great Empires and the immense prospects of spoils thus opened up. Not merely a redistribution of the spoils of Africa but a renewal of the far more important competition for the control and development of China occupy the vision of the keen-eyed financiers and business groups who, when they choose, control the foreign policy of every country.

Thus in the last resort international politics is mostly business and is therefore penetrated by the emotions and beliefs of the business world, not taken as a whole but ranged in national groups and interests. Now, as we have already seen, the doctrine held in common by individualist free-traders and by socialists, that industry and commerce are, or should be, essentially processes of human co-operation in the benefit of which all must be sharers, is not the operative principle in the actual political economy of nations. In most industrial countries the statesmen correctly embody in their protectionist-imperialist policy the conviction of the great majority of business men that trade is essentially competitive in its international aspect, in the sense that the commercial progress and prosperity of other nations are injurious to our own. This doctrine, driven home, we showed to rest upon a belief, well-founded under existing conditions, that there was not enough market to keep everybody busy all the time. This belief we found inspiring the policy of ca' canny among workers, the organisation of trusts and combines for regulating output among employers, while it is alike the intellectual support of Protectionism in every country and the evident and avowed motive of Modern Imperialism. But the operation of the reparations policy is the most convincing evidence to-day, of the paralysing influence of the limited market. We simply cannot produce because Germany by the lower costs (i.e. sweating) we have forced upon her, occupies too much of this limited market. Our more enlightened financiers, economists, and statemen, are hastily fumbling round for means to expand this market, so as to make it possible for the idle mills, mines and workers to get to work. All the practical schemes turn on the creation of reliable credits, and this means either an augmentation of purchasing power which shall give more immediate effective demand for goods to persons who will spend it in buying them. But the aggregate market can only be thus expanded in so far as the credits operate to raise consumption among the low-consuming populations and classes. No one would suggest applying credits to stimulate shipbuilding or the building of woollen mills at the present time. The folly of adding to the unemployed plants in such industries would be too obvious. On the other hand, credits applied to promote the production of ploughs and steam-engines to be exchanged in Roumania, or in more fertile provinces of Russia, for foodstuffs to raise the consumption of starving or underfed peoples in the Volga or other depleted areas, would react in a genuine increase of production, both here in the trades doing this export trade and in the countries which received these ploughs and engines. As regards the emergency provisions for unemployment in this country, it is pretty clear that in a general trade depression it is folly to set men working in their trades. Either they must be set on public works that could not otherwise be undertaken then, or in default of these, they must be provided with food, clothes, etc., or the means to buy them. Either course means a stimulation of effective demand for commodities, and, so far as it goes, reacts in stimulation of production of these articles along the various direct and indirect channels of production in this and other countries. The only cure for under-production is more production; but this cure can only operate on condition that the distribution of the ownership of the increased product is such as to evoke increased consumption. All these credit schemes turn in the last resort on this condition.

The special character given to the present cyclical depression by the destructiveness of war must not be allowed to conceal its fundamental economic nature and to furnish support to false remedies. The material destruction of the War was not so great but that it could by this time have been completely repaired, had a good peace been made without delay, accompanied by a vigorous international policy for dealing with the temporary dislocations of trade, transport and finance. The failure to do this is responsible for the special character and intensity of this depression, and has brought the world-economic system into so feeble a functioning as to keep current production so low that the margin of current saving is reduced to a minimum. I wish to make it quite clear that my general charge of oversaving as the root-cause of fluctuations and depressions is quite consistent with the admission that during a deep depression there is under-saving in the sense of a rate and proportion of saving to spending inadequate to the normal needs of a progressive industry. It is often said at such a time as this that there is a shortage of capital. This, however, is not strictly true. Taking the structure of industry as a whole, it is demonstratively false, for almost all forms of capital exist in apparent superabundance. There are, however, now, as at all times, certain new industries or other developmental work which might function if cheap abundant new capital were available. Such capital is not available, because current production and therefore current real incomes are so low that saving has shrunk to its lowest proportions. Business profits have in most cases disappeared, taxation presses on all classes, and the great majority of the people have not the economic power, even if they had the will, to effect further economies in their current expenditure.

Unemployment, springing in the last resort from a distribution of purchasing power which gives too much to classes who have their pressing wants already satisfied, can only be remedied by a transfer of some of this purchasing power to the poorer classes who will apply it to satisfy felt wants.

I believe that the special war and post-war policies so frequently adduced to explain how this depression differs wholly from ordinary cyclical depressions can all be shown to bear testimony to this constant defect in our economic system which always works towards gluts and depressions.

II

An intelligently acting individual in economic isolation, a Crusoe, or a completely inclusive economic society, would maintain a just balance between the amount of energy devoted to the satisfaction of immediate wants and that devoted to preparation for the satisfaction of increasing future wants. But this intelligent economy of spending and saving need not apply to single members of an economic group, or to particular groups within some larger society. Particular members of a self-sufficing group may cut down their current consumption to any dimensions consistent with physiological survival, provided that other members of the group will make good their personal economy by consuming more. It is a group balance that must be maintained between production and consumption.

This implies that in an international economic world there is no necessary limit to the current savings of a particular nation. If it saves more than the right proportion imposed by the prevailing condition of the arts of industry, it can make good that excess by enabling some other nations to save less. In other words, it may continue to roll up increasing claims upon other peoples, postponing indefinitely the enlarged consumption which these claims enable it to practise. This is what the great creditor nations of the world have to various extents been doing, ever since industry evolved to the point of producing surpluses beyond those utilisable as capital to supply the rising home consumption. Great Britain was doing this before the War, investing larger proportions of its surplus savings abroad and not even receiving for home consumption the full interest upon past investments. The United States has recently been practising the same economy with concentrated energy. During the War her surplus savings were poured into Europe, enabling the belligerents hugely to expand their 'consumption' while reducing their production. After the War American lending continued on a vast scale, by further advances and reinvestment abroad of most of the interest due. Indeed, the new drive of American business into export trade, coupled with her rigorous Protection, involves the assumption of the rôle of creditor on a larger scale than any other country has yet undertaken. The policy of indefinite postponement of satisfactions to which a people is entitled seems absurd, and would be impossible if it represented the conduct of a people as a whole. But if we envisage large amounts of surplus class income, carrying no appreciable satisfaction from current expenditure, and therefore rolling up into automatic savings whose interest is subjected to a similar accumulation, we can understand how this group control of savings and investment may bring about a long continued career of increasing creditorship. One nation may thus be induced and enabled to save an indefinitely large proportion of its income, provided other nations are thereby induced to spend more and save less.

It sometimes appears as if there were no limit to the proportion of the world-income that might be saved except what may be termed the physiological limit of subsistence. For there is, it is contended, no limit to the amount of useful new developmental work that may be set on foot with a view to enlarged production of future commodities. But this is also true of Crusoe. If he is fool enough, he may work so hard in making precarious preparations for the future that he gets no satisfaction out of the present. But as an intelligent man he sets a right limit upon this process of postponing present and more certain to future and less certain satisfaction. And the world as a whole is in the position of Crusoe. As far as it is guided by reasonable self-interest, it will limit the proportion of the saving to its spending, not deferring present satisfaction to an excessive extent in order to promote capital undertakings which may never mature in future increase of commodities, or which, if they do, may be rendered futile by a continued refusal to expand consumption fast enough to give full employment to the increase of productive power. Unfortunately there yet exists no organised intelligent will of the world to ensure the operation of this economic policy.

If, however, it be admitted that, while there is a limit to the reasonable rate of saving for investment on the part of the economic world as a whole, no such limit seems to be binding on any particular nation, or other group, there arises the practical consideration whether the provisions against unemployment, by better distribution of the income between capitalists, wage-earners and the State, can be made effective in a world so imperfectly developed for purposes of international control. Such political or economic measures as may be taken for regulating excessive profits, or for diverting them to purposes of public revenue, or for securing a better distribution of the product as between capital and labour, are almost entirely confined to particular national areas.

Now the extension of modern capitalist production to a larger and larger number of nations, all of whom by their improved mechanical resources contribute to the fluctuations and depressions, may appear to render any purely national action almost futile, or even injurious. Suppose, for example, that England alone pursued the policy of correcting her proportion of saving to spending, by diverting to increased wages and increased tax revenue the surplus incomes of the rich, so far as it was effective in securing a better application of the national income, it could not sensibly diminish the depressions which are brought upon us by world-gluts and price movements. Though a country tolerably self-sufficing for production and investment might find substantial relief from the liability to trade depressions by a better internal adjustment of production and consumption, this could not be the case for any country largely dependent upon world markets and foreign investments. For a country like Great Britain, accustomed in recent times to invest as much as half its annual savings overseas, no merely national solution is feasible, and the same reasoning applies to most great industrial countries with an ever-increasing pressure. At present the violence and the uncontrolled nature of external movements of commerce and finance are driving most nations to seek the shelter of tariffs, subsidies and other barriers against economic internationalism. But this emergency policy cannot long prevail against the forces which make persistently and ever more powerfully for international co-operation. This signifies that no sound solution can be found for any of the great economic problems affecting standards of production, distribution and consumption, except by a policy which is in effect if not in express contrivance international.

Applying this criticism to the large problem here set out—the better correlation of rate of production and rate of consumption by means of better distribution of the product—we have to ask how far a tendency towards such improved distribution can be discerned in the world-economy. I have already cited some factors in the problem, so far as our national economy is concerned. But it is evident that no confident judgment can be formed upon the wider issue. For there are very few countries in which reliable statistical evidence of the distribution of incomes exists, enabling us to judge whether the surplus income, whose excessive accumulation is the main source of trouble, forms an increasing or a diminishing proportion of income as a whole. To set out upon such an inquiry is no part of my purpose here. But it may not be out of keeping with that purpose to indicate some general considerations bearing on this important matter.

Whether the economic experiences of the war have made for or against the equalisation of incomes and absorption of the surplus, it is not easy to decide. One of its most patent results has been a large increase of the aggregate of the interest charge in most of the belligerent countries. Subscribed in every country mainly from the war profits of the rich, the burden of the new war debts hangs heavy on the industrial peoples of the world. Every further fall of prices, of course, increases the size and the proportion of this addition to the surplus income of the rich. The temporary rise in rate of interest for new capital may not add much to the net income of the capitalist class, implying as it does a less amount of supply of new capital. But the impetus given by war economy to the organisation of businesses into combines, and other non-competent and price-controlling bodies, definitely strengthens their surplus earning power.

On the other hand, as we have seen, certain counteracting forces, political and social as well as purely economic, strengthening the position of the workers must be taken into account. In all great industrial countries the numerical strength of trade unionism has been growing. The temporary failure of organised workers to retain, during the present depression, the whole or the bulk of the wage-gains made during the war must not be allowed to obscure the substantial advances made, particularly by the lower grades of workers. Organisation, politics and public sentiment contribute to sustain a definite rise in standard of living for the workers in these countries.

The growing liberty of migration from country to town, from poorer and less developed countries to richer and more developed ones, has been, notwithstanding legal, social and other barriers, continually drawing larger numbers of workers into environments, where higher standards of living have been established and where better organisation of workers for pressing their economic claims and interests is practicable. Even before the War it was generally agreed that part of the rise in prices of important foods and raw materials was to be attributed to the increasing proportion of world-workers found in countries, like the United States, with a high standard of living, and to the successful demand for a rising standard, especially of food, in large sections of the working populations of India, Japan, China and other backward countries entering upon careers of modern industrialism. This progressive migration from areas of lower standards of consumption to areas of higher standards is not in itself conclusive proof of a better general adjustment between production and consumption, for the higher consumption thus attained might be accompanied by a more than corresponding rise in production. But there is reasonable ground for holding that the breakdown of long-established habits of low conservative consumption achieved by migration to a new and more progressive environment, together with the greater capacity for collective bargaining and political assistance in securing higher standards, has enabled the working-classes to obtain a larger proportion of the product, the real income of the economic world, than they had heretofore. This tendency is doubtless offset in some measure by increasing opportunities for the temporary exploitation of new immigrants into industrial countries and of backward peoples in their own countries by profiteering capitalism. But since the necessary implication of such exploitation of weaker groups is to stir in them new demands which crave economic satisfaction, it seems likely that the general result is some movement towards equalisation of incomes, in the sense that the surplus available for automatic accumulation forms a smaller proportion of the world income. This, of course, is by no means certain. It might be that the Western civilised Powers would, by separate or conjoint policy, fasten upon the undeveloped countries and their unresisting populations so rigorous an economic domination as would draw from them a surplus real income large enough, not only to buy off by private concessions and public subsidies class discontent within their borders, but to retain upon the wider scale that inequality of income which causes periodic congestions of goods with ensuing depressions. If capitalism can keep firm hold of national and international policy, this new phase, in which whole Western nations become parasitic upon the weaker and the backward peoples of Asia and Africa, may be practicable. If, however, this economic imperialism which has made such rapid advances during the past few generations is successfully combated by the extension of a liberal equalitarian and humanitarian policy from the narrower field of national democracy to the relations between advanced and backward peoples, some gradual solution of our problem may be found in a rising standard of world consumption.

There are those who hold that nothing short of international socialism is capable of achieving this result. If so, there seems little prospect of any early escape from or abatement of our economic troubles. If, however, I am right in holding that some movement towards equalisation of incomes is afoot within most of the advanced nations, an increasing proportion of surplus being diverted into wages or intercepted for public services, it seems reasonable to hope and expect that the same conjunction of economic, political and moral forces which has been working for this equalitarianism within each nation may be operative on the wider international scale. The new experiments in constructive internationalism might make very serviceable contributions to this end. A new body, at present feeble but capable of growth and activity, has been provided for that international labour movement which hitherto has been little more than an exuberant aspiration. Intergovernmental agreements to promote common standards of work and life for the workers of different nations should help to raise the general standard of distribution within the several nations towards the level of the highest. The regulations laid down in the Covenant of the League of Nations for the economic dealings of its members with the peoples of mandated areas, though at present perhaps little more than the formal tribute which imperialism pays to liberty, attest at least some real advance among the more enlightened classes of the Western nations towards considered regard for the welfare of subject races, and may grow into a genuinely authoritative code of international conduct, if this moral and political enlightenment prevails over the forces of national selfishness and short-sighted cupidity. I will not prejudge the victory in the struggle between the powers of light and darkness. But if the influences which are able to curb the excesses of capitalist domination within the civilised modern state can be brought into effective bearing on the wider area of internationalism, imposing partly by the moral power of public opinion, partly by intergovernmental action, economic rules for the protection of the interests of weaker peoples and in particular for securing for them an adequate share of the product of their labour, the world market and the world consumption should be able to escape the constriction of the past and to expand with sufficient facility and pace to furnish full and regular employment to the world's productive powers, however fast they may themselves advance with every fresh improvement in the arts of industry.

CHAPTER X

A SUMMARY

THE following summary of the argument contained in these chapters may be useful in helping readers to form a clear judgment upon its validity.

The existence of a normal tendency for the rate of industrial production in the world to outrun the rate of consumption of commodities, i.e. the existence of a limited market, is attested by common experience in the business world. This belief is admittedly a chief cause of restriction of output, as practised by workers and by capitalist combinations, and furnishes the chief support of protective tariffs and imperialist policy. This normal failure of consumption to keep pace with actual and potential production is manifestly responsible for the periodic gluts, stoppages, under-production and unemployment, which precede and constitute cyclical depressions. Misapplication of productive power, as between one group of industries and another, one area of industry and another, though responsible for much waste, will be a fairly constant factor in the complex world-economy, and cannot be regarded as a chief cause of the accumulating general gluts which usher in cyclical depressions. Nor is there any reason to suppose that meteorological fluctuations, affecting world-harvests, are competent to account for the size and the nature of the phenomena of trade depressions. There is only one sort of maladjustment of economic forces adequate in nature and magnitude to explain the actual phenomena, viz. a normal tendency to apply to the production of capital-goods a proportion of the aggregate productive power that exceeds the proportion needed, in accordance with existing arts of industry, to supply the consumptive-goods which are purchased and consumed. In other words, if there exists a normal tendency to try to save and apply to capital purposes an excessive proportion of the general income, we have a valid explanation of the actual phenomena of fluctuations and depressions.

Now in the wide disparities of income between the rich and poor, and in the large elements of unearned and unneeded income which fall to the former class, we discover the required tendency to chronic over-saving, i.e. the virtually automatic accumulation of income which exceeds the customary or desired expenditure of those whose felt wants are fully satisfied. Under such conditions it is certain that the proportion between spending and saving must get out of gear, and that more production will be applied to producing larger increases of plant, raw materials and other capital goods, than are capable of full and regular use in furnishing consumable goods to consumers.

The economic checks commonly adduced, viz. the falling rate of interest as a check upon excessive saving, and the fall of prices as a stimulation of increased consumption, are both inadequate. Neither operates until the trouble has attained considerable momentum, or is effective until great waste and damage have occurred.

For these periodic movements of over-accumulation of capital over-production, congestion of the machinery of industry, stoppages and unemployment, with their slow unloading of excessive stocks, there can be no real remedy except a removal of the surplus elements in large incomes which brought about the disproportion between saving and spending.

The progressive movement in the economic life of the industrial nations is, in effect, though not of clear purpose, largely directed to this end. The absorption of the unearned and unneeded incomes of the rich, partly by the rising wages and standards of living of the workers, partly by the needs of a modern State, tends to bring about that equalisation of incomes which is essential to a natural and right adjustment between the proportions of spending and saving in the aggregate income. This absorption of surplus and the higher rate of consumption it secures do not involve a deficiency of saving or a lack of capital for the enlarged needs of future consumption. The present depressions signify a feeble and wasteful operation of the excessive amount of capital brought into existence. The better distribution of income here envisaged, though involving a reduced *proportion* of saved income to spent, would not involve a less *amount* of saving. For the fuller and more regular working of the machinery of industry would produce a real income so much larger than the present that a smaller proportion of saving would yield a quantity of new industrial capital at least as large as heretofore. Nor would the necessary incentives to such saving be lacking in the new order.

If by such improvements in distribution the rates of production and consumption were so well adjusted as to reduce to small dimensions the fluctuations of employment, the largely superstitious influence of confidence and credit in the causation and enlargement of these fluctuations would tend to disappear. For the regularity of actual business operations, thus obtained, would be reflected in a steadiness of prices precluding the swift enlargements and contractions of credit which stimulate and exaggerate our cyclical fluctuations. For if the actual industrial system were kept in regular and full employment by the removal of restrictions in the market, speculation and expansion of credit would be confined to narrow limits. Once remove the opportunities which the conjunction of rising prices and unemployed productive resources afford to business men and financiers of reaping large and quick gains from getting control of large stocks in a rising market, you destroy the demand for inflated credit and the over-confidence engendered in the atmosphere of business speculation.

The roots of irregularity and fluctuation of industry lie in defects of distribution and of demand, not in the miscalculations of business men or the aberrations of the monetary system, which are but exaggerated reflections of the real facts of industry.

Considerations of the enfeebled and confused condition in which the Great War and the Bad Peace have left the industrial, commercial and financial system of the world, impair no whit the validity of this analysis or of the remedies which it discloses. The temporary breakdown of production over large areas of Europe and the low consumption in these areas, which are the most serious economic and human aspects of this emergency, have, of course, greatly enlarged, as they have also given special shape to, the general depression. These war wounds to our economic system call for emergency measures. But these measures are of the nature of first aid, and must not be regarded as substitutes for the remedial treatment which deeper diagnosis of the disease demands. If Reconstruction successfully achieved meant setting again on its old legs the economic system of the past, we should continue to stumble at brief intervals into the same ditch and, wading through much dirt, danger and discomfort, emerge again weakened in body and confused in mind to pursue once more the same perilous uncharted journey.

I have here approached the economic problem from the single path of trade depression, and have shown that a solution of the problem can only be found by such economic, social and political reforms as secure a drastic redistribution of the product of industry. If we are to get industrial security, peace and progress, that redistribution must be achieved. If State Socialism, or Guild Socialism, or Consumers' Co-operation, or any form of Communism, can achieve this better distribution, without unduly letting down production, we may look for salvation along any of these paths. But if, as I am disposed to believe, no people is prepared to launch in any wholesale way on any of these revolutions, some mixed policy of national ownership of prime monopolies, control of profits, prices and conditions of employment in other industries where some measure and degree of direct or indirect competition survives, with a limited period of free profitable enterprise as an incentive to new enterprises—the whole of this linked up by a tax system whereby society secures for beneficial public services the idle elements of income which do not nourish or evoke productive effort—this mixed policy adapted to the varying conditions in the world of industry will best achieve the better and more equal distribution and utilisation of income that are required.

APPENDIX

PROTECTION AND THE LIMITED MARKET

THE reason why a general trade depression is so dangerous to free trade is that under this condition the ordinary simple refutation of the case for a protective tariff in the *immediate* interests, not merely of a particular trade but of a particular nation, will not work.

Let us test it by an illustration. At a time of general unemployment in most of the staple industries here and on the Continent, a British railway is considering two tenders for the supply of rails, one from Belgium, one from Glasgow —the former being at a slightly lower price. Now the free trade judgment is absolute in favour of the Belgian rails, as against the protectionist plea for the employment of the idle capital and labour at Glasgow. The free trader argues, not only that it is advantageous to the railway to buy the cheaper foreign goods, but that this course will not reduce the total volume of employment in this country. For, he contends, the purchase of the Belgian rails by English money must, operating through the usual channels of exchange, cause a demand for British export goods which would not otherwise have taken place. There will, he contends, be extra work for otherwise unemployed workers in Northampton, Leicester, Birmingham, etc., to make the goods which go out to pay for the Belgian rails. And it is clear that more employment in the export trades of this country will result from buying the Belgian rails. But does this mean that the total volume of employment in this country will be greater? The protectionist may reply: If the rails are bought from Glasgow instead of Belgium, the same goods which would have gone to Belgium (or their equivalent in other goods) will have to go to Glasgow to pay for the rails made there. The export trade will, indeed, be less than it would have been, but the total trade and employment within this country will be greater, because it will contain the making both of the rails and of the other goods which the Glasgow workers will be able to demand as the result of the employment they receive. It is, of course, the familiar argument which Adam Smith adduced under the rather perverse title of " the Two Capitals," urging that there was a prima facie case for preferring internal to foreign trade, because both transactions in the process of exchanging goods against goods were kept inside the same political area. This argument will not, I think, hold water under ordinary trade conditions, in which the available productive power of a country may be considered to be fully employed. Under this condition it is evidently better to buy in the cheaper foreign market, for no total increase of employment will result from preferring the home-made goods. But where there is general unemployment both in this country and abroad, the immediate case for employing otherwise unemployed British capital and labour is far more plausible. " Yes, plausible, perhaps, but not sound," some free traders will certainly reply. A very able English exponent of free trade, the late Mr. Russell Rea, contended that the difference between foreign and internal trade, due to the difference of methods of payment, was such as to invalidate the statement that if the Glasgow rails were bought instead of the Belgian, the same demand for British labour to pay for them would take place. He insisted that the purchase of the Belgian rails stimulated a production of British export goods in payment, for which there would be no equivalent if the purchase of the rails were an act of internal trade. Now I am quite unable to admit that the foreign exchange, operating in one case and not in the other, alters the essential fact that the purchase of the rails enables and impels the recipients of the price to use their purchasing power to demand the production of other British goods. In the one case, the Belgian employers and workers who, otherwise, on our hypothesis of unemployment, would remain idle, will have a job and must spend the money they receive (or cause other Belgians to spend a corresponding sum) in a demand for British goods. In the other case, the Glasgow employers and workers, otherwise idle, will have the job and the money, and will spend it in demand for about the same amount of British goods. The fact that the methods of payments are slightly different is irrelevant to the issue. It is curious that it should be necessary to point this out to free traders. For the most fundamental principle of free trade is that a political barrier has no proper significance at all in the sound economy of trade. For the economic international society, to which both British and Belgians belong, it is clearly advantageous that the rails should be bought in the cheaper market, though it means less unemployment in Belgium and more in Britain, but it is foolish to shirk the stark and obvious fact that, if a British railway has the option of setting to work unemployed Glasgow steelworkers on the one hand, or Belgian unemployed steelworkers on the other, the immediate effect of taking the former course is to increase the aggregate employment in this country. The Glasgow workers will buy as much other British produce by the money they receive, and buy it as soon, as would the Belgian workers, and this act of purchase will have the same stimulating effect upon other British trades in both cases. This is quite manifest, if omitting the machinery of payment we confine our attention to the substance of the trade in question. However the payment is effected, what the railway really buys the rails with is the carrying services which it performs. This process of exchanging transport against rails involves no doubt some intermediaries. Probably in neither cases, whether the rails are bought in Glasgow or in Belgium, will the actual railmakers take their payment directly in the transport service of the railway. The railway will sell transport to various British manufacturers and traders, who will pay for it in goods sent to Glasgow or Belgium for consumption by the railworkers in one of these places. However many intermediary processes of sale may take place, the ultimate fact issues that the railway pays for rails in terms of transport, and there is no ground for supposing that the Belgian purchase sets more capital and labour to work at an earlier time than would the Glasgow purchase. The same amount of employment is brought about. The difference is that in the one case part of the employment takes place outside this country, in the other case it does not. Viewing the transaction quite objectively, one may prefer the Belgian purchase, on the ground that, while it makes no appreciable difference in the volume of world employment, it is better for the railway to buy in the cheaper market, and it conduces to the better economy of the world that the cheaper or more efficiently conducted business should get the job.

There is, of course, another consideration present to some of your minds which, for simplicity of argument, I have kept back for separate consideration. If the British railway has to pay appreciably more for Glasgow than for Belgian rails, its running costs and freight rates must be raised. This rise of freight might be so considerable as to cripple trade and so strike back at production and employment in the general industry of the country. Such general damage to employment through railway costs might more than outweigh the increased employment given to Glasgow railmakers. On the other hand, if the price difference between the Belgian and the Glasgow tenders were very small, the net result of preferring Glasgow might be a smaller amount of unemployment in this country and a larger in Belgium.

In other words, given a general depression and unemployment in the industrial world, a tariff might be used to distribute the aggregate volume of employment for the time being favourably to the political area which set it up. In the case adduced, a tariff keeping out Belgian rails might, if it did not raise considerably the price of British rails, cause more employment in this country. This judgment is, in reality, only an extension of the common admission that, if a special local trade could keep a special pull upon a tariff, so that its workers gained more as favoured producers than they lost as consumers, their plea for protection had rational validity. On a short perspective, it seems probable that during a general trade depression, a skilfully wielded tariff might shift part of the burden of unemployment on to other political areas. I need hardly add that no mortal tariff would be either skilful or honest enough to keep within the limits of the economy, watching the comparative costs of production in the various countries so closely as to prevent organised industries inside the tariff area from raising prices so high as to cause more unemployment than it cured.

I spoke just now of a short perspective. As a lasting policy such a defence of national employment could not succeed. There would emerge two inevitable causes of failure. The first is primarily political. As in the case of protection for infant industries (quite defensible on theoretic lines) the fatal objection is that such infants never grow up, so here the temptation to retain this fiscal remedy for unemployment during normal trade conditions, so as to force disproportionate amounts of capital and labour into certain favoured industries and keep them fully furnished with lucrative orders at the expense of the general body of national trade, would be irresistible. Now the injurious effect of such a policy is obvious. It would offend the first principle of productive economy by forcing into certain avenues of employment capital and labour which could find more productive occupation elsewhere. The total wealth of the community would thus be diminished by spreading the same aggregate of employment in a more wasteful manner. In other words, it is only the recurrent phenomenon of general trade depression which gives specious validity to a tariff as a mitigation of unemployment.

The other fatal flaw in the policy, except on a short range expediency, is economic. It will be admitted, by all free traders at any rate, that the broad effect of any tariff, even under the circumstances here described, must be to force capital and labour to be less productively employed upon the average than if left to the undiluted play of free international trade and investment. This means that such action as we contemplated for the exclusion of Belgian rails would cause rails to be made more expensively in Britain by employing capital and labour in that country than by employing these factors of production in Belgium. If this simple case be expanded into the dimensions of a protective policy, designed primarily to keep the maximum of employment in the protected country, it must fail. For capital employed under these conditions will be less productively and less profitably employed than if it went abroad to Belgium or elsewhere where it was free to utilise cheaper or more efficient labour. The inevitable result of such a protective tariff would be to stimulate the export of new capital from this country, so leaving a reduced supply for the development of our internal industries. The reduced employment for labour thus brought about would stimulate the emigration of workers to countries where the supply of capital and of employment had been made more abundant by the operation of this tariff. The only way of preventing this reduction of her volume of employment in this country would be by preventing or penalising the export of capital, a policy actually proposed by certain persons who favour the imposition of a discriminative tax upon incomes derived from foreign investments. But this attempt to keep capital at home, less productively and less profitably employed, would mean a reduction of the average yield of capital, and a consequent, though perhaps not proportionate, diminution of saving for investment. It is important to recognise that an integral and necessary part of a protective policy is this compulsory retention of capital in the protected area, and the consequent reduction of the rate of interest and of the creation of new capital.

Only by putting a sort of ring-fence round a country to stop its capital and labour from flowing abroad in search of more productive uses, as well as to stop foreign goods from entering its frontiers, could protectionism make the appearance of a case for safeguarding employment. Now it is one thing to restrain the export of capital and labour during a brief war emergency, when governmental work ensures full remunerative employment for all of both factors, quite another to erect these restraints into a normal policy, even for dealing with periods of cyclical depression. The conclusion of my argument is this. If it were the sole object of economic statecraft to cause the largest quantity of work to be done within the national area, irrespective of the quantity of wealth produced and the standard of living, a protective policy of this more rigorous order might, if it were confined to periods of general depression, achieve this result. In other words, it is theoretically possible to keep an artificially inflated amount of employment within a favoured area, were it practically feasible or otherwise desirable. A state, in other words, could make its working population *ascripti glebæ*, keeping them employed at home under a lower standard of production and consumption than they would attain under conditions of *laissez faire laissez aller*.

PRINTED IN GREAT BRITAIN
BY UNWIN BROTHERS, LIMITED
PRINTERS, LONDON AND WOKING

Titles in This Series

1. H. L. Beales and R. S. Lambert, eds. MEMOIRS OF THE UNEMPLOYED. 1934

2. A. L. Bowley and Margaret H. Hogg. HAS POVERTY DIMINISHED? 1925

3. Marian Bowley. HOUSING AND THE STATE 1919–1944. 1945

4. Henry Noel Brailsford. SOCIALISM FOR TODAY. 1925

5. H. N. Brailsford, John A. Hobson, A. Creech Jones, and E. F. Wise. THE LIVING WAGE. 1926
   bound with
   R. Palme Dutt. SOCIALISM AND THE LIVING WAGE. 1927

6. BRITAIN'S INDUSTRIAL FUTURE. 1928

7. A. M. Carr-Saunders and D. Caradog Jones. A SURVEY OF THE SOCIAL STRUCTURE OF ENGLAND & WALES. 1927

8. G.D.H. Cole. THE NEXT TEN YEARS IN BRITISH SOCIAL AND ECONOMIC POLICY. 1929

9. G.D.H. Cole and M. I. Cole. THE CONDITION OF BRITAIN. 1937

10. Hugh Dalton. PRACTICAL SOCIALISM FOR BRITAIN. 1935

11. Ronald C. Davison. THE UNEMPLOYED: OLD POLICIES AND NEW. 1929

12. M. P. Fogarty. PROSPECT OF THE INDUSTRIAL AREAS OF GREAT BRITAIN. 1945

13. Arthur Gleason. WHAT THE WORKERS WANT: A STUDY OF BRITISH LABOR. 1920

14. Wal Hannington. THE PROBLEM OF THE DISTRESSED AREAS. 1937

15. John Hilton. RICH MAN, POOR MAN. 1944

16. J. A. Hobson. THE ECONOMICS OF UNEMPLOYMENT. 1922

17. S. G. Hobson. NATIONAL GUILDS AND THE STATE. 1920

18. E.M.H. Lloyd. STABILIZATION: AN ECONOMIC POLICY FOR PRODUCERS & CONSUMERS. 1923

19. C.F.G. Masterman. ENGLAND AFTER THE WAR. 1922

20. The Pilgrim Trust. MEN WITHOUT WORK. 1938

21. G.C.M. M'Gonigle and J. Kirby. POVERTY AND PUBLIC HEALTH. 1936

22. Sir George Newman. THE BUILDING OF A NATION'S HEALTH. 1939

23. THE NEXT FIVE YEARS: AN ESSAY IN POLITICAL AGREEMENT. 1935

24. Sir John Boyd Orr. FOOD, HEALTH AND INCOME. 1936

    bound with

    Sir John Boyd Orr and David Lubbock. FEEDING THE PEOPLE IN WAR-TIME. 1940

25. OUR TOWNS: A CLOSE UP. 1943

26. Eleanor F. Rathbone. THE DISINHERITED FAMILY: A PLEA FOR THE ENDOWMENT OF THE FAMILY. 1924

27. William A. Robson, ed. PUBLIC ENTERPRISE: DEVELOPMENTS IN SOCIAL OWNERSHIP AND CONTROL IN GREAT BRITAIN. 1937

28. William A. Robson, ed. SOCIAL SECURITY. 1943

29. B. Seebohm Rowntree. POVERTY AND PROGRESS. 1941

30. E. D. Simon. HOW TO ABOLISH THE SLUMS. 1929

    bound with

E. D. Simon. REBUILDING BRITAIN—A TWENTY YEAR PLAN. 1945

31. John Strachey. REVOLUTION BY REASON. 1925

32. Richard M. Titmuss. POVERTY AND POPULATION. 1938

33. Richard Titmuss and Kathleen Titmuss. PARENTS REVOLT. 1942

    bound with

    Richard M. Titmuss. BIRTH, POVERTY AND WEALTH. 1943

34. George Walworth. FEEDING THE NATION IN PEACE AND WAR. 1940

35. Whiting Williams. FULL UP AND FED UP: THE WORKER'S MIND IN CROWDED BRITAIN. 1921